The Japanese Short Staff

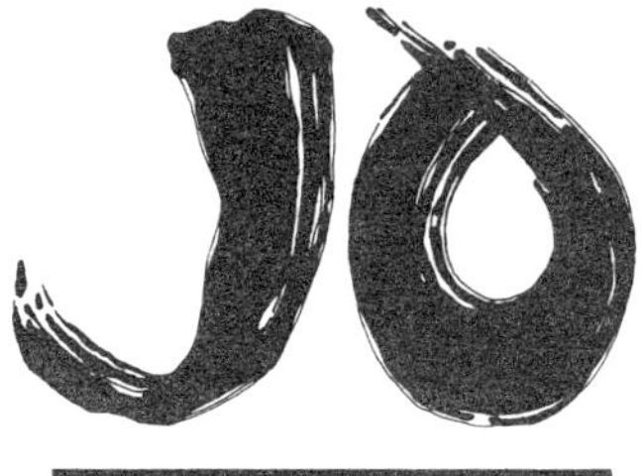
JO

The Japanese Short Staff

By Don Zier and Tom Lang

Unique Publications

ISBN: 0-86568-058-2
Library of Congress Catalog Card Number: 84-52443

Unique Publications, Inc. www.cfwenterprises.com
4201 Vanowen Place
Burbank, CA 91505

DISCLAIMER

Please note that the publisher of this instructional book is NOT RESPONSIBLE in any manner whatsoever for any injury which may occur by reading and/or following the instructions herein.

It is essential that before following any of the activities, physical or otherwise, herein described, the reader or readers should first consult his or her physician for advice on whether or not the reader or readers should embark on the physical activity described herein. Since the physical activities described herein may be too sophisticated in nature, it is *essential that a physician be consulted.*

Book Design: Danilo J. Silverio

To Yoshio Yamaguchi, Edward van Dyke, and Harold the Upright,
for their patience and inspiration.

CONTENTS

INTRODUCTION

In this book we present 22 traditional short forms *(suburi)* and two long forms *(kata)* for the Japanese short staff *(jo)*. These forms preserve and teach the basic principles of fighting with the short staff.

We have designed this handbook for students receiving instruction with the jo. While a careful reader could, we hope, grasp the fundamentals of the jo without assistance, we stress that there is no substitute for personal instruction. Instructors of the jo should be familiar with most of these techniques and should incorporate them in their teaching at some time.

Because a book is only as good as the reader's understanding of it, we have paid special attention to the presentation of information and have sought to explain techniques rather than simply to record them. The pages are arranged to present a long sequence of photographs and accompanying text without interruption. The photographs were taken from the same angle to preserve the continuity of each form. Supplementary photographs at different angles are included where appropriate. Each photograph includes a reference line to show the length and direction of each step, and many have arrows that show the path of the jo or the motion of the body. The text is brief and concise and is followed by a glossary of Japanese terms.

1. THE JO

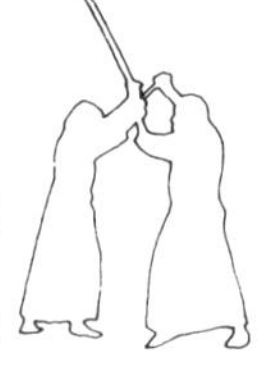

The jo is made of hardwood and averages about 50 inches in length and 7/8 of an inch in diameter. It is round or octagonal in cross section. These dimensions are not critical to the techniques in this book, although a staff of approximately this size is preferred. For practice with a partner, a staff of standard length is desirable. For practicing alone, a staff long enough to pass just underneath your armpit when standing is adequate.

The jo is sometimes called the *four-foot staff* or the *short staff* to distinguish it from the *long staff* or *rokushaku bo* (literally, six-foot stick), and the *three-foot stick* or *hanbo* (literally, half-stick).

The history of the jo includes a divine birth and a noble heritage. It begins in the early 1600s, when a samurai named Muso Gonnosuke meditated in the mountains after his first and only defeat, at the hands of Japan's greatest swordsman, Miyamoto Musashi. (In classical Japanese, the last or family name precedes the first name. Muso and Miyamoto are family names.) Muso's favorite weapon was the *bo*—the long or six-foot staff. Miyamoto, using both a long and a short sword, had blocked the staff in such a way that Muso could not withdraw his weapon safely. Miyamoto spared Muso's life, however, and left him to meditate on his defeat.

The result of Muso's meditation was a "divine insight" that led him to develop a shorter staff and a style of fighting with it. He called his style *shindo muso ryu jojutsu,* and with it, he defeated Miyamoto in a second dual. He, too, spared his opponent's life and became the only man ever to best the master swordsman.

1

2

Figs. 1 and 2 Jodo evolved from jojutsu, which was developed to work against a sword or another staff. The entwining techniques shown here are typical of jodo.

Muso's impressive success with the jo is in part the result of the nature of the weapon. It is from six to eleven inches longer than the sword, and while a jo can break a highly tempered blade, a sword cannot cut through a one-inch-diameter oak jo (although a cut can render the jo useless as a weapon). The length of the jo also permits numerous hand changes and turnovers that involve both ends in the actions of thrusting, striking, sweeping, receiving, and entwining (Figs. 1 and 2). Thus, jojutsu is a dynamic, versatile, and effective fighting art, although it never achieved the importance of the sword arts.

Because it was developed to use against swordsmen, jojutsu is heavily influenced by sword techniques, particularly in striking, fencing postures, and receiving actions. The jo is also a pole arm, however, and incorporates the thrusts, sweeps, entering motions, and receiving actions of the spear *(yari)* and halberd *(naginata)*.

Eventually, the martial arts of the battlefield became the martial ways of the training hall, and combat-effective "external" disciplines became character-building "internal" ones. Just as *jujutsu* (grappling) became *judo*, and *kenjutsu* (sword fighting) became *kendo*, jojutsu became *jodo*, although jodo still retains most of its combat orientation.

Jodo deals expressly with disarming and subduing an opponent armed with one or two swords or a jo. Entwining and *atemi waza* (striking vulnerable points of the body) are integral parts of the training (Fig. 3).

The jo was also adapted by Uyeshiba Morihei, the founder of *aikido*, to teach the principles of aikido. His use of the weapon is called *aikijo*. Aikijo resembles jodo in that both involve fencing with the jo, but differs in the nature and purpose of the fencing. Jodo techniques are often faster and sharper because angular attacks and defenses are part of its combat orientation. Aikijo techniques are slower and softer because circular movements can blend attacks and defenses and reduce the attitude of conflict (Fig. 4). Inserting and entwining techniques are not found to the same extent in aikijo as they are in jodo, nor are the numerous targets of atemi waza. Aikijo does have jo-taking and jo-keeping techniques, but these are aikido throws in which the jo is incidental to the throw rather than essential to it. Thus, while aikijo is more limited than jodo because it has fewer targets and fewer kinds of movements, it is also much broader in that its application does not depend on a four-foot staff but on the fundamental movements of aikido.

From the staff forms preserved in many martial traditions, we selected those that most closely resemble the forms available from various instructors in the United States today. We did not preserve a particular tradition of staff fighting; rather, we chose basic thrusting, striking, sweeping, hand-changing, single-hand, forestalling, and receiving techniques to create a balanced introduction to the use of the jo.

Fig. 3 Striking the wrist is one of many *atemi waza*, or strikes to vulnerable points of the body. Such strikes are commonly found in empty-handed as well as in weapons arts.

Fig. 4 Aikijo emphasizes "soft" or blending and receiving actions. Here, the thrust is simply guided to the side rather than knocked out of line.

Traditional instruction in the Japanese martial arts proceeded from solo exercises *(suburi* and *kata)*, to paired practice *(kumijo)*, to free-style sparring *(randori)*, to fighting *(shiai)*. Instruction in the weapons arts proceeded from handling the weapon, to attacking and defending against the same weapon, to attacking and defending against different weapons and unarmed opponents. Here, we begin the instruction process with forms that teach the student how to handle the jo and how to attack and defend against an opponent also armed with a jo.

Practice forms—suburi and kata—are the "museum pieces" of the martial arts: they are not technique, they preserve technique. A stuffed tiger is not a tiger, but one can learn something about "tigerness" from studying it. (Actually, you can only learn about "stuffed-tigerness," but it's still a good analogy.) In the martial arts, this means that suburi and kata teach the principles of combat: timing, focusing, awareness of openings *(suki)*, and awareness of distance *(maai)*. Fighting with the jo involves the dynamic application of these principles. Only through practice will you learn how to apply the principles through appropriate actions.

The jo, then, is a humble weapon with a noble history; a simple weapon capable of great complexity. The fundamentals of its use have been preserved in—and sometimes hidden in—numerous forms. This book is directed to the study of these forms.

2. CONVENTIONS AND TERMS

We use two conventions in describing the forms. First, we refer to an opponent about your own size who is also armed with a jo. This convention allows us to describe a technique by identifying a target for you to hit or an attack you will receive. When practicing alone, you must imagine your opponent, the targets he presents, and the attacks he makes.

The second convention, used in the photographs, is a *reference line* that is the initial line between you and your opponent. It is drawn on the floor and is shown with a hatchmark that indicates where your weight should be centered at the beginning of each technique. The reference line appears in each photograph so that the length and direction of each step may be shown.

An imaginary *line of attack* also exists between you and your opponent. This is the path along which a jo must travel to hit a target. When you are directed to "move out of line," we mean you should move out of the line of attack to avoid being hit. The line of attack is often parallel to the reference line, especially at the beginning of a technique. As you or your opponent move, however, the line of attack also moves and is no longer parallel to the reference line.

The jo is referred to as having an *end,* which is the end that hits the target, and a *butt,* which is the end that does not.

The *forward hand* is closest to the end of the jo; the *back hand* is closest to the butt. The *forward foot* is closest to your opponent; the *back foot* is farthest away.

An *action* is a specific and purposeful movement of the jo. Here, the actions are thrusting, striking, sweeping, and receiving.

A *hand-change* is a change in the position of your hands on the jo. In a *simple* or *sliding hand-change,* the jo is allowed to slide through your grip. In a *single* or *double hand-change,* your hand(s) leave the jo and regrip at a different place.

An English description follows the Japanese name of each form. The descriptions are not necessarily translations. Translations may be found in the glossary.

3. PRELIMINARY SKILLS

Gripping

Effective thrusts, strikes, sweeps, and receiving actions with the jo require you to transfer the power of your body to the jo and, hence, to the target. Your grip is important in transferring this power; it must not weaken or break on impact.

The jo is gripped in the same way as the sword and other pole arms. The last three fingers of each hand surround the shaft and press it to the palms. The thumb folds over the top of the middle finger (Fig. 5). Occasionally, the angle of the jo requires that this grip be relaxed, in which case the thumb and index finger hold the shaft (Fig. 6).

Posturing

The forms in this book begin with one of two postures. Each lends itself to different attacks and defenses, but both allow you to bring the jo into play quickly and effectively.

Fig. 5 To grip the jo correctly, squeeze the shaft to your palm with the last three fingers of each hand. Keep your thumb and index fingers relaxed and roll them into the shaft.

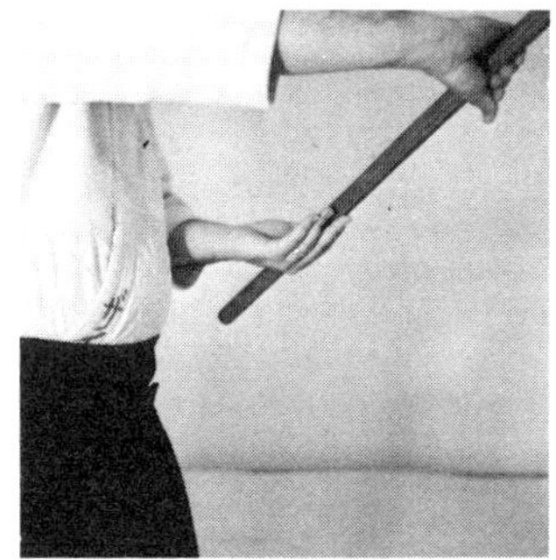

Fig. 6 Your grip may sometimes shift to the thumb and index finger if the angle of the jo makes it impossible to grip with the last three fingers.

SIDE VIEW

FRONT VIEW

Fig. 7 The *sankakutai* posture.

SIDE VIEW

FRONT VIEW

Fig. 8 The *chudan no kamae* posture.

The first posture is *sankakutai* (Fig. 7). Stand in a left T-stance on the reference line: your left foot should point to your opponent along the reference line; your right should be turned 60 to 90 degrees to the right and be from one to two feet behind your left. Stand relaxed with your knees flexed and your weight centered between your feet over the hatchmark. Your hips and shoulders should face about 45 degrees to the right. Let your right arm relax at your side. Hold the jo vertical, with your left hand about waist-high on the shaft and the butt on the reference line a little in front of your left toes.

Sankakutai is a good posture from which to thrust and is a traditional posture for the jo and other pole arms.

The second posture is *chudan no kamae* (Fig. 8). Stand in a right T-stance and center your weight as before. Your knees should be flexed. Position your hips, shoulders, and arms as directed in Figures 9 through 11.

Chudan is a traditional fencing posture for the sword arts of kendo and iaido and is important in delivering effective strikes. You may find it awkward at first.

Two other traditional fencing postures occur in the forms. *Jodan no kamae* (Fig. 12) is a threatening posture in which the jo is held ready to strike. In *hasso no kamae* (Fig. 13) you shoulder the jo in preparation for a variety of moves.

Two more traditional fencing postures occur incidentally in the forms; we include them for completeness. *Gedan no kamae* (Fig. 14) is like chudan, save that the jo is held down rather than up. *Waka no kamae* (Fig. 15) is taken from hasso no kamae by simply lowering the jo behind you.

Fig. 9 To assume the chudan posture, square your hips to the reference line and point the jo upward, with your right hand about 12 inches above the butt. If your hips are square, your left hand can reach as far up on the shaft as your right hand.

Fig. 10 Now, turn your hips to the left. This will draw your left arm across your chest and your left hand will slide toward the butt of the jo. When your left hand reaches the butt, your hips and shoulders should be in the correct position and will face about 45 degrees to the left of the reference line. Your right arm is now "longer" than your left in that it can reach farther along the reference line.

Fig. 11 Hold the jo directly above the reference line, in front of and away from your body, and point it at your opponent's face. You are now in chudan.

Moving

Good training forms teach good movement. That is, good suburi and kata are built on the principles of good body mechanics; to perform them well, you must learn to move efficiently, not just smoothly or quickly. Moving efficiently means accomplishing a given movement without wasting energy. It also means transferring the power of your body through the jo and into your opponent with the minimum loss of power so that you deliver as powerful an action as possible.

We distinguish two kinds of movement: *General movements* are large, obvious movments, such as stepping, turning, striking, thrusting, and so on. General movements are easy to duplicate after you have seen them once or twice. *Precision movements* are specific, refined movements that combine to make the larger, general movements.

For example, the general movements of, say, a sword cut, are striking out and down with the arms; the precision movements—how the cut is performed—are the specific motions of the right arm pushing out, the left arm pulling down, the wrists "wringing" the hilt, the elbows losing their splay, and so on.

Because they are so subtle, precision movements are not easily recognized or learned. They are the most important aspect of movement; they are the key to efficient actions. They are also the movements most often lost as forms are passed from teacher to student.

One reason why precision movements are lost is that few movements are produced as they appear to be produced. That is, the part that moves is usually moved by some other part of the body. For example, to step forward with your right foot, you have to straighten your left knee. The right foot moves, but the left knee does the work. So, if your right foot is not in the right place at the right time, the problem is most likely in your left knee. Likewise, the elbows control the hands. If your hands are not moving correctly, check the position of your elbows throughout the movement.

Fig. 12 The *jodan no kamae* posture.

FRONT VIEW

Fig. 13 The *hasso no kamae* posture.

FRONT VIEW

Fig. 14 The *gedan no kamae* posture.

FRONT VIEW

Fig. 15 The *waka no kamae* posture.

FRONT VIEW

The knees control the hips as well as the feet. A general task in any martial art is learning how to keep from "floating," that is, from losing your balance. Floating can be prevented (or at least postponed) by keeping the knees flexed. If the knees are where they should be, the hips will be properly positioned.

The arms and legs have different but complementary functions. For example, the direction and reach of a strike are controlled by the placement of your feet, not by turning your upper body or by "reaching" with your arms. Often, when your hands control the height of the jo, as in a receiving action, your feet will control the horizontal distance between the jo and your opponent. Similarly, when your hands control the horizontal distance of the jo, as in a thrust or jab, your legs may control the height of the jo through standing or kneeling. If each part of your body moves as it is supposed to, the result will be coordinated, efficient movement. If your form feels or looks awkward, you may be using the wrong part of your body to produce the movement.

4. BASIC ACTIONS

The forms described in this book involve four basic actions: thrusting, striking, sweeping, and receiving. Suburi demonstrate the different forms of these actions, and kata show how to move effectively from one action to another. Before we present the suburi and kata, a word is in order about the basic actions of thrusting, striking, sweeping, and receiving.

Thrusting

Definition

A *thrust* is the action of driving the end of the jo into the target. We identify an *underhand thrust,* in which the forward hand is palm-up and the back hand is palm-down; an *overhand thrust,* in which both hands are palm-down; and a *reverse-hand thrust,* in which the jo is held at face level with the forward palm facing away from you and the back palm facing you. We also distinguish between a *thrust,* which is powered with one hand, and a *jab,* which is powered by two.

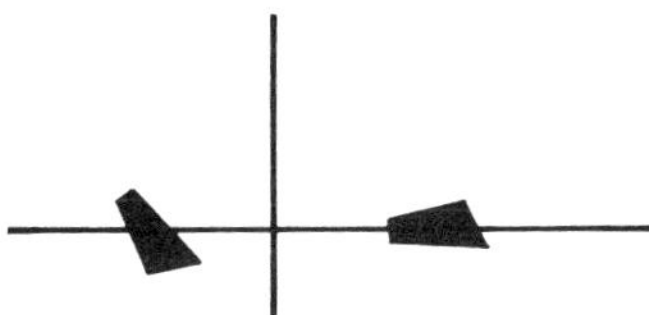

Fig. 16 In a left T-stance, center your weight over the hatchmark on the reference line.

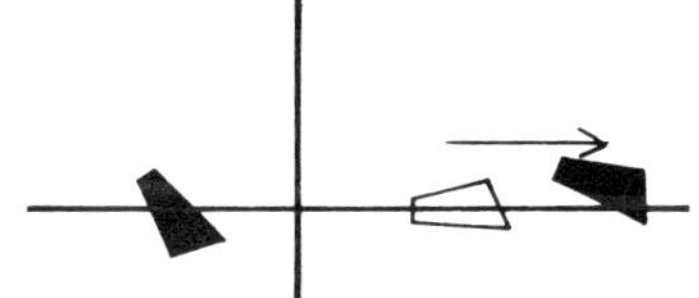

Fig. 17 Advance your left foot, toe first, and let your weight come down behind your knee.

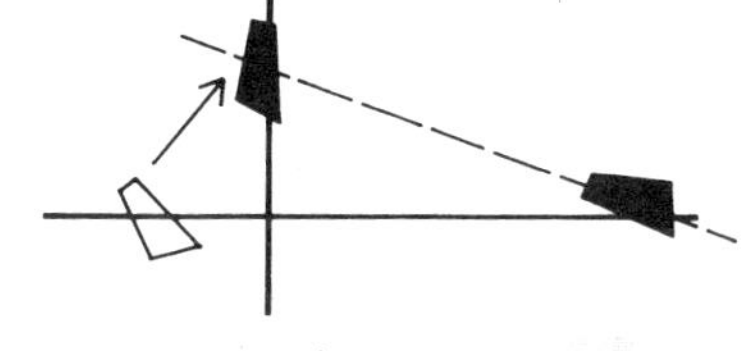

FRONT VIEW

Fig. 18 Slide your right foot to the left, and let some of your weight drop down, not forward, as you complete the thrust.

Description of General Movements

Figures 16 through 18 show an underhand thrust to the chest. The overhand thrust is the same, except for the position of your hands. The reverse-hand thrust is explained when it appears as a suburi.

Stand in a left T-stance and hold the jo horizontal, with your left hand about 18 inches from the end, your right hand at the butt (Fig. 16). Assume your opponent faces you in the same stance. Advance your left foot eight to twelve inches along the reference line. As you step, let your weight come forward and down behind your left knee and onto your toes (Fig. 17). As your weight leaves your right foot, slide it ten to twelve inches to the left of the reference line and thrust the jo forward with your right arm. When you thrust, extend your left arm and let the jo slide across your left palm. Some weight should drop to your right foot as you thrust. The jo should stay horizontal during the thrust but may be lifted naturally by the motion of your arms (Fig. 18). Stop the thrust when your right elbow comes to your side.

Discussion of Precision Movements

Feet and knees. Stepping forward with your left foot establishes the aggressiveness of the action and puts your weight behind the thrust. To step, shift most of your weight to your right foot by bending your right knee slightly. As your weight shifts, you will feel as though your right knee is taking the weight. Do not attempt to shift your weight by keeping your right leg straight while pushing off with your left foot; this will cause you to float. When enough weight has shifted, slide your left foot forward; it must not move back.

Straighten your right knee and bend your left knee to shift your weight to your left foot. Set your weight on your toes—not on your heel—for better control. If you step correctly, your left knee will flex, and you will be able to spring back from the step by pushing with your toes (Fig. 19). This is more difficult if your weight is on your heel because the movement of your ankle cannot help control the spring (Fig. 20). When enough weight has shifted, slide your right foot to the left of the reference line. To stop both the slide and your forward motion, bend your right knee and let some of your weight shift to the ball of your right foot. Time the impact of your thrust so it will occur at this point.

Hips. Before you thrust, your hips should be turned at about 45 degrees to the reference line. The side step pulls your right hip to the left so that after the step your hips are nearly parallel to and to the left of the reference line. Because your opponent thrusts along the reference line, the side step takes your hip out of his line of attack. When your right foot accepts weight after the side step, your hips will drop a little. If you have correctly alternated the

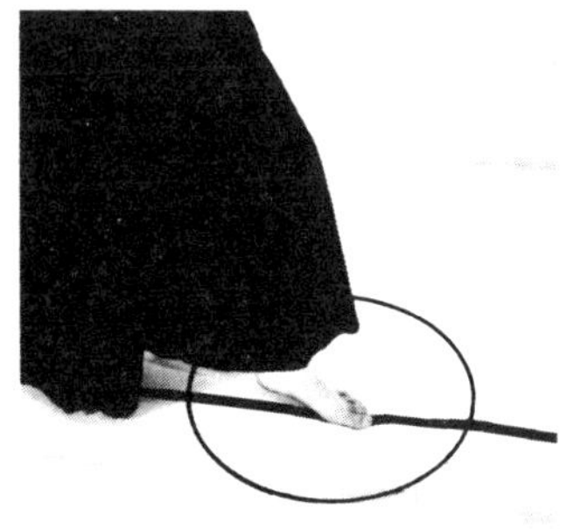

Fig. 19 When you step, put your weight on your toes. You can bounce out of the step with the movement of your ankle as you push with your toes.

Fig. 20 If you put your weight on your heel, you will have to bounce out of the step by extending only your knee and not your ankle. This reduces your stability in recovering from the step.

bending and straightening of your knees, your hips will move as they are supposed to, and you will not float.

Back. Keep your back straight throughout the thrust.

Chest and Shoulders. Your chest and shoulders move with your hips.

Arms and Hands. As you thrust with your right arm, open your left hand and support the jo across your palm (Fig. 21). In the overhand thrust, you will

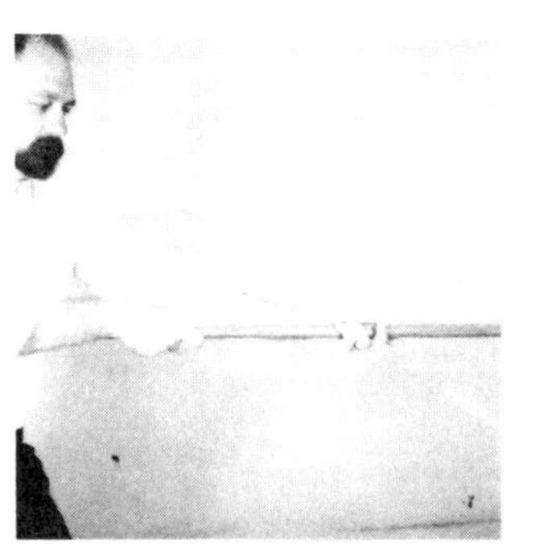

Fig. 21 Correct hand position at the end of an underhand front thrust.

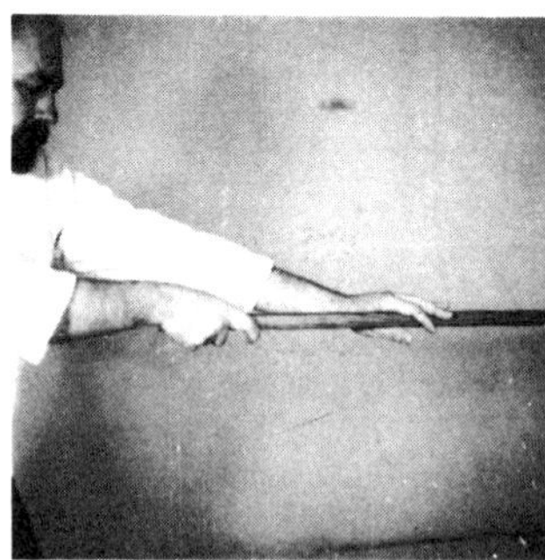

Fig. 22 Correct hand position at the end of an overhand front thrust.

support the jo across your left thumb (Fig. 22). As you extend your left arm, the jo will lift naturally, and you can thrust to your opponent's chest rather than to his waist. Power the thrust entirely with your right arm and stop when your right elbow comes to your side. Tighten your left grip at impact to stabilize the thrust.

Keep your right wrist directly over the jo. If your wrist were to one side, a strong downward push on the end of your jo could break your grip on the butt by bending your wrist.

You can improve the accuracy of your thrust if, instead of trying to guide the end of the jo to the target, you watch the target and think of pushing your right hand to your left along the shaft.

Common Mistakes

Figures 23 through 26 illustrate some common problems with the thrust. Figure 27 shows the correct position at the end of the thrust.

Fig. 23 Your left foot should point to your opponent, not to the right.

Fig. 24 Your weight should be behind your knee, not over it.

Fig. 25 Your back foot should slide to the left, not forward.

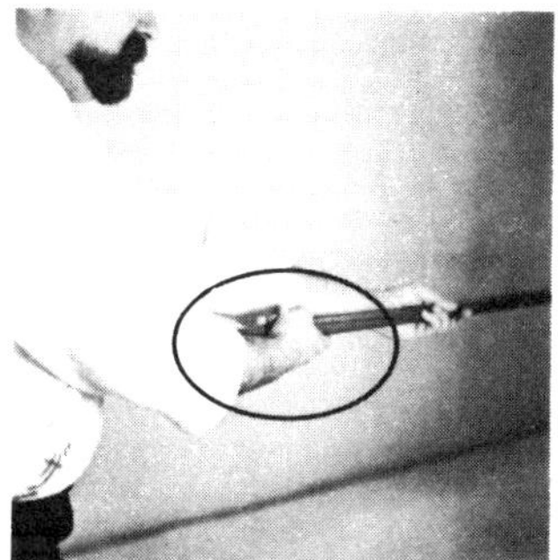

Fig. 26 Your right wrist should be directly over the jo, not to the side.

Fig. 27 Correct position at the end of a front thrust.

Striking

Definition

A *strike* is the action of swinging the jo in a more or less vertical arc to hit the target from above. We identify a *shomen strike,* which is a vertical strike (usually to the top of the head), and a *yokomen strike,* which arcs about 30 degrees from the vertical (usually directed to the side of the head). The yokomen strike has both a right- and a left-handed form.

Description of General Movements

Figures 28 through 32 show a shomen strike. From chudan (Fig. 28), raise your arms over your head as if you were pushing the jo up and back, so that the jo points behind you (Fig. 29). Splay your elbows as you raise your arms. Swing your arms down sharply to complete the strike. As your arms swing down, eliminate the splay of your elbows by extending your arms and by "wringing" the jo with your hands. This puts your wrists behind the jo so that they can withstand the impact of the strike (Figs. 30 through 32). Your left arm powers

SIDE VIEW

Fig. 28 Begin in chudan.

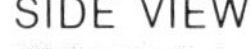

Fig. 29 Raise the jo over your head and bend your back knee to shift your weight to your back foot. Push the jo up with your left hand.

SIDE VIEW

Fig. 30 Swing your arms down. Your left powers the jo, your right guides it.

the strike and swings down as it extends. Your right arms directs the strike and pushes out as it extends. The strike stops naturally when your right arm is fully extended (Fig. 32). As you strike, let your right knee accept some weight so that your hips will drop and add your weight to the strike.

Discussion of Precision Movements

Feet and Knees. Your left foot is stationary throughout and provides a stable foundation for the strike. Your knees alternately bend to shift your weight, first back and then forward. Your right foot may slide a little toward your left foot as your weight shifts back. This motion is reversed for the actual strike: your right foot slides forward on the toes to accept your weight, which is brought down behind your knee. If you emphasize stepping with your toes and bending your right knee, you should be able to step in and back quickly for a number of strikes.

Hips. Your hips should face about 45 degrees to the left of the reference line throughout the strike. Your weight should shift forward and down to your right knee as you strike.

Fig. 31 Begin to "wring" the jo to bring your wrists behind it.

Fig. 32 Feel the jo extend just before completing the strike. Let your weight come down behind your right knee as you complete the strike.

Fig. 33 Your left hand swings in an arc that, if continued, would pass by your left hip. Your right hand pushes out, toward your opponent. You should feel the jo stop naturally as your right arm becomes fully extended. Because your right hand is pushing out and your left is swinging down, you will feel as though you are stretching the shaft between your hands.

Back. Keep your back straight throughout the strike.

Chest and Shoulders. Your chest and shoulders should be parallel to your hips and face about 45 degrees to the left of the reference line. You may find this awkward at first, but it positions your arms for an effective strike.

Arms and Hands. The strike involves three separate motions of your arms and hands. The first is the obvious motion of swinging your arms down, particularly the left arm, which provides most of the power for the strike. Your left arm should swing down in an arc that, if continued, would pass by your left side. Your right hand directs the strike by pushing the jo toward your opponent (Fig. 33).

The second motion of the strike is the "wringing" motion of the hands that puts your wrists behind the jo so that they can withstand the impact of the strike. Your thumbs should rotate toward each other, as if you were wringing a dish towel to dry (Fig. 34). Hold the jo firmly in your left hand and let the shaft rotate in your right until both wrists are in position. Tighten your right grip just before impact. The wringing motion accompanies the extension of your arms and the corresponding elimination of the splay of your elbows.

The third motion is a "whipping" or "extension" of the jo that occurs just before impact. Remember that in the chudan posture, your right arm is "longer" than your left; that is, it is farther forward than your left. In jodan, however, your right arm is behind your left. As long as your right hand is behind or even with your left hand, the jo swings in an arc centered at your shoulders. When your right hand passes you left during the strike, it pushes the jo into a second arc centered at your left hand. This second arc produces the whip (Fig. 35).

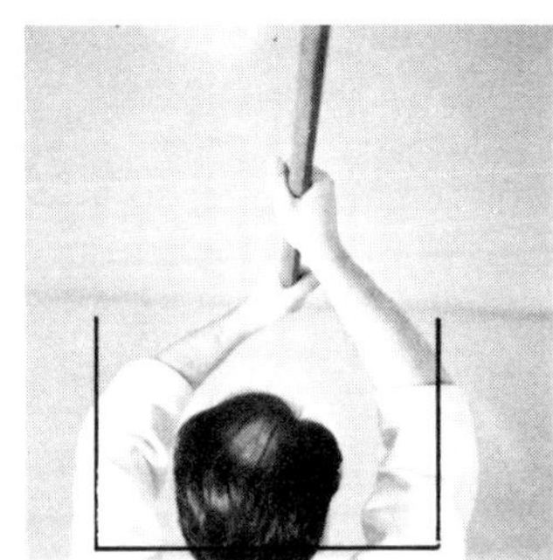

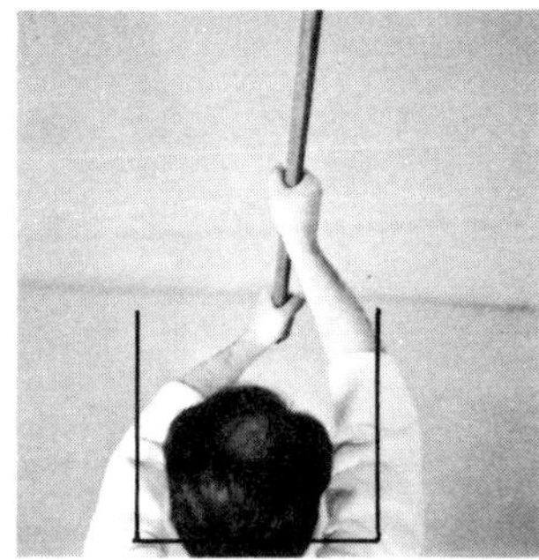

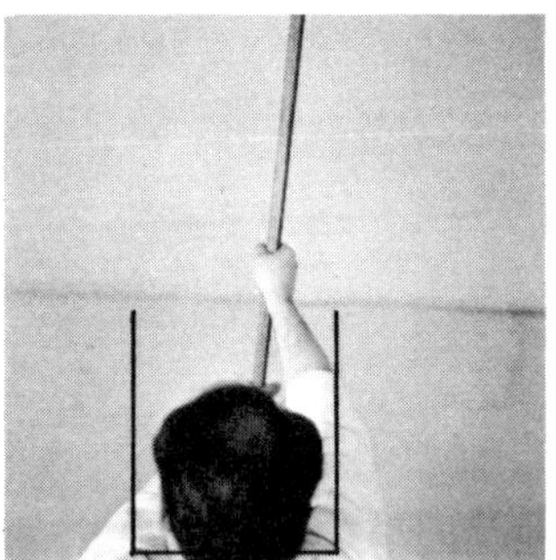

Fig. 34 When you extend your arms to eliminate the splay in your elbows, bring your wrists behind the jo as if you were wringing the shaft. Hold the jo firmly in your left hand and let your right hand slide around the shaft until both wrists are in position. Tighten your right grip just before impact.

Fig. 35 The strike is composed of two arcs. The first is the obvious one of the arms swinging down. The second is produced by the right hand as it pushes the jo past the left and is the result of having the shoulders turned to the left to offset the reach of the arms. The first arc centers at the shoulder. The second, which produces the extension, centers at the left hand.

The strike is stopped naturally when the right arm reaches full extension. As the strike stops or makes contact with the target, everything comes together: the three arm motions, the step with the right foot, and the dropping of the hips. The combined effect is an efficient, powerful strike.

Yokomen Strikes

The *right-handed yokomen strike* is virtually the same as the shomen strike. Tilt the jo about 30 degrees to the right by moving your right hand to the side. Your left wrist will turn clockwise. Move your arms as before, with the same three motions used in the shomen strike, but adjust the angle of the jo to a position from which you can strike to the side of the head. (Figs. 36 through 39).

A

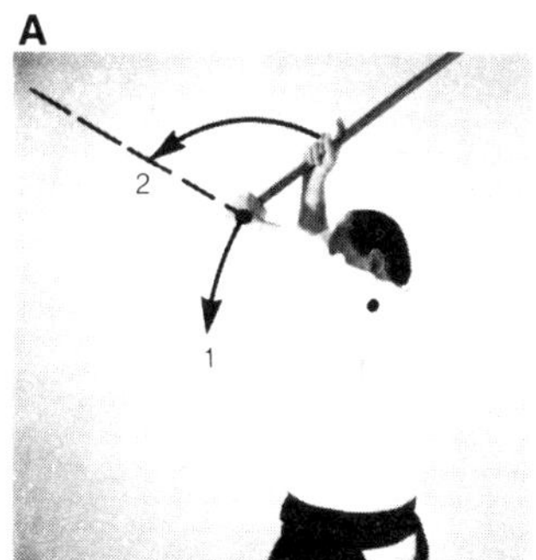

B

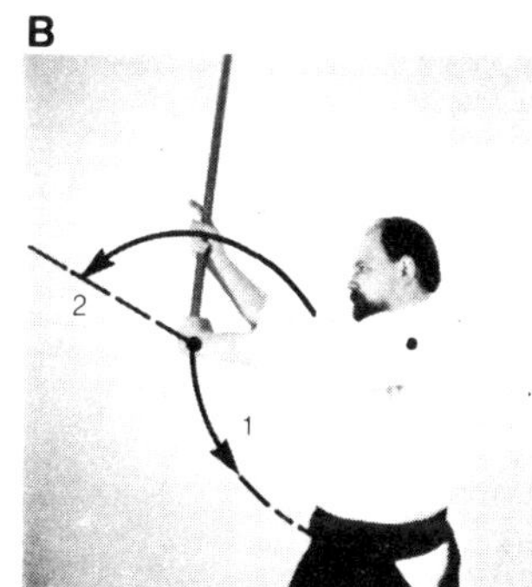

C

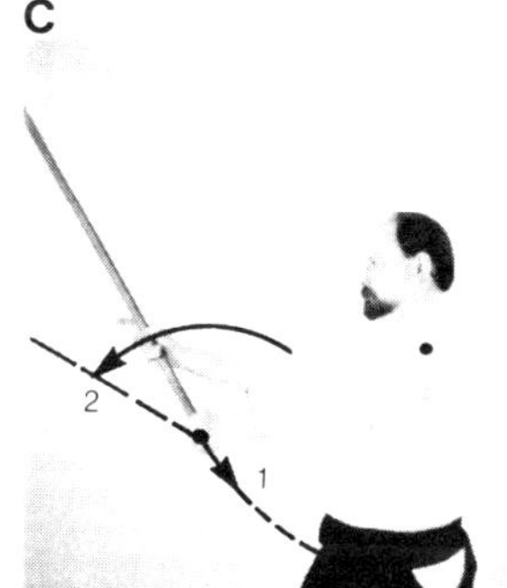

D

The *left-handed yokomen strike* also employs the same principles of striking, but looks a little different. It is executed with the left foot forward, and strikes 30 degrees to the left of the vertical. This means that your arms cross in front of you and you must adjust the angle to a position from which you can strike to the side of the head (Figs. 40 through 42).

Common Mistakes

Figures 43 through 47 illustrate some common problems with the strike. Figure 48 shows the correct position at the end of a shomen strike.

Figs. 36 through 39 The right *yokomen* strike slants about 30 degrees to the right of the vertical and is usually directed to your opponent's left ear.

36 **37** **38** **39**

Figs. 40 through 42 The left yokomen strike slants about 30 degrees to the left of the vertical and is delivered with the left foot forward. It is usually directed to your opponent's right ear.

40

41

42

Fig. 43 Your weight should be behind your knee, not over it.

Fig. 44 Your right hand should be pushed out, not swung down.

Fig. 45 The strike should end with your wrists behind the jo, not to the sides, and with your elbows straight, not splayed.

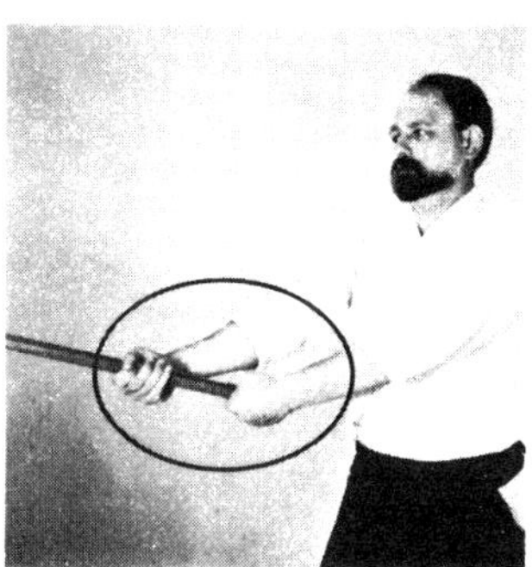

Fig. 46 Your wrists should be straight, not bent.

Fig. 47 Your shoulders should be turned to the left, not square.

Fig. 48 Correct position at the end of a *shomen* strike.

Sweeping

Definition

A *sweep* is the action of swinging the jo in a more or less horizontal arc to hit the target from the side. We identify an *overhand sweep,* in which both hands grip palm down, and a *reverse-hand sweep,* in which the hand at the butt is palm-up and the other palm-down.

Description of General Movements

Figures 49 through 53 show an overhand sweep. Stand in a left T-stance and hold the jo palms down. Your left hand is at the butt and the jo is pointing behind you, past your right side. Your left hand is close to your right hip, and the jo is parallel to the reference line (Fig. 49). Sweep the jo around by pulling your left hand across your waist to your left hip and walk forward with your right foot into a right T-stance. Power the sweep with your left hand and direct it with your right. Your left hand turns over a little as you sweep, which causes the jo to rotate in your right hand. Let it rotate, and tighten your right hand just before impact. The jo should not continue past your opponent but should end roughly parallel to, and to the left of, the reference line.

Discussion of Precision Movements

Feet and Knees. The footwork in the sweep moves you from a left T-stance into a right one. Bend your left knee to shift your weight from your right foot until

Fig. 49 Center your weight over the hatchmark and hold the jo behind you.

Fig. 50 Pull you left hand around your waist from hip to hip and begin to step forward with your right foot. Cock the jo as you begin to step.

Fig. 51 Power the jo with your left hand and guide it with your right.

Fig. 52 Begin to add your hips to the sweep.

you can step. Point your right foot at your opponent when you step and let your left foot pivot into position. Your weight should come down on your right foot just before you hit the target.

Hips. Your hips turn counterclockwise as you step and should contribute to the power of the sweep. Set your weight down behind your right knee after the step.

Back. Keep your back straight throughout the sweep.

Chest and Shoulders. Before the sweep, your shoulders have shifted clockwise from your waist to hold the jo in position. They snap counterclockwise during the sweep as you pull your left hand across your waist and push with your right palm. At the end of the sweep, your shoulders are turned about 45 degrees from the reference line. The sweep stops as your hips finish their turn and as your shoulder begins to bind from pulling the end of the jo to your left hip.

Arms and Hands. Your right wrist should be straight and should come behind the jo as you sweep to be in proper position for withstanding an impact. Your left hand should grip firmly throughout the sweep. Since this causes the jo to rotate during the sweep, your right hand must let the shaft turn in the grip until just before impact, or your right wrist cannot come behind the jo (Fig. 54). This is similar to the "wringing" motion of your hands that occurs in the strike.

The reverse-hand sweep (Fig. 55) is similar to the overhand sweep, although it is not as powerful. Your left hand is palm-up and must come up to your left shoulder during the sweep. This reduces your extension and limits the sweep

SIDE VIEW

FRONT VIEW

Fig. 53 Feel your weight come down on your right foot just before you complete the sweep.

Fig. 54 Correct hand position for the overhand sweep.

Fig. 55 Correct hand position for the reverse-hand sweep.

to the ankle or knee. Again, your left hand grips the jo firmly throughout the action, and your right lets the shaft rotate until just before impact.

Common Mistakes

Figures 56 through 58 show some common problems with the sweep. Figure 59 shows the correct position at the end of an overhand sweep.

Receiving

Definition

A *receiving action* is the action of protecting yourself by intercepting your opponent's jo to change the direction or timing of his attack. We identify a *beat,* in which you strike your opponent's jo sharply from his line of attack, and a *deflection,* in which you redirect his jo with a push.

Description and Discussion

Specific receiving actions are too numerous and varied to describe in general motions. Rather, we describe them as they appear in the forms. We can say something, however, about the general functions of receiving actions.

A receiving action should effectively thwart an attack and should leave you in a position to counterattack. The *deflection* changes the direction of the attack by pushing your opponent's jo up, down, or sideways. It is an efficient and common receiving action because only a small push is necessary and because your opponent's jo need be redirected only enough to clear your

Fig. 56 The sweep should not swing around but should stop just past the reference line.

Fig. 57 Your left wrist should be straight and directly above the jo at the end of the sweep, not bent and to the side.

Fig. 58 Your left hand should stop in front of your left hip, not behind it.

Fig. 59 Correct hand position at the end of an overhand sweep.

body. The end of his jo often passes beyond you, which gives you the advantage because you will be inside his attack, in line, and ready to counterattack.

The *beat* is a receiving action. It can disrupt the timing of an attack by accelerating your opponent's jo along the line of attack (this takes away his initiative), or it can disrupt the action of his attack by sharply knocking his jo out of position. The beat is more vigorous than the deflection and is supposed to break the continuity of your opponent's attack without breaking you own. This will become clearer as you progress through the forms and see specific receiving actions.

A receiving action is often accompanied by movements that take you out of your opponent's line of attack or that adjust the distance between you and your opponent. These movements involve turning, retreating, and lifting. These are precision movements and their purpose is not always clear to students practicing alone. It is important, therefore, to remember the purpose of movements, or your practice will become sloppy and the movements will be lost.

5. TARGETING

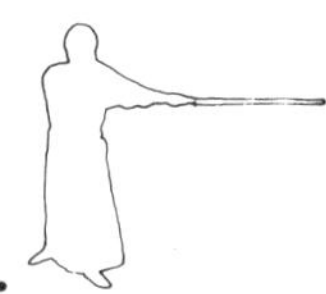

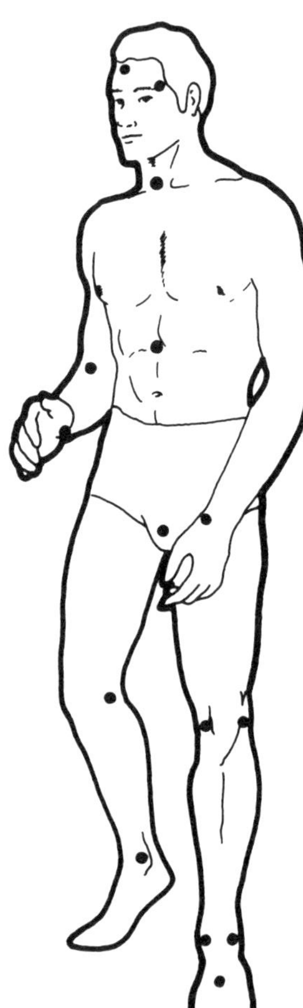

Fig. 60 Common targets for striking with the jo.

Part of the combative application of the jo is *atemi,* the art of striking vital points *(kyusho)* on the body of an opponent to disable him. Atemi strikes can produce pain, temporary paralysis, structural damage to the body, unconsciousness, or death, depending on: the point struck; the intent, force, and precision of the attack; the size and physical condition of the opponent; and in some cases, the timing of the attack with respect to the opponent's breathing cycle. The most common targets attacked with the jo are charted in Fig. 60 and are described below.

Tento (the point of the forehead) is most easily attacked with a shomen strike.

Kasumi (the temples) are usually attacked with yokomen strikes and occasionally with high sweeps.

Uto (the point between the eyes) is usually attacked with high jabs or thrusts.

Jinchu (the point under the nose) is usually attacked with high jabs or thrusts.

Sonu (the throat) is usually attacked with high jabs or thrusts.

Suigetsu (the solar plexus) is a major target for thrusts.

Hiji (the elbows) are usually attacked with high sweeps when the opponent's arms are raised.

Tekubi (the wrists) are most easily attacked with high sweeps when the opponent's arms are raised and by strikes when his arms are lowered.

Hokashiyakuzawa (the back of the hands) are most easily attacked with high sweeps when the opponent's hands are raised, and with strikes when they are lowered.

Kinsho (the testicles) are a less common target for the jo but are occasionally attacked with an upward sweep.

Hiza (the knees) are usually attacked with sweeps and occasionally with kneeling strikes. Both the inside and the outside of the knees are vulnerable to attack.

Kurabushi (the ankles) are almost always attacked with sweeps.

Kori (the tops of the feet) are usually attacked with thrusts or jabs.

6. TIMING

Definition

Timing is the coordination of two or more movements to produce the maximum effect. We identify an *internal timing* among the movements of your body and an *external timing* between your actions and those of your opponent.

Description and Discussion

Timing is an important principle in any martial art, for timing is essential to precision, and precision is essential to good technique. Timing is one of the subtle differences between the dynamic, flowing movements of the instructor and the memorized, mechanical ones of the student. Timing is difficult to develop because it is so subtle that only continued concentration brings it into awareness, and because it is easy to compensate for a lack of it.

Internal Timing

Well-delivered actions depend not only on correct movements, but on timing these movements so that the full effect of each is felt precisely at the moment of impact. This means that all your movements should be focused at the point at which you hit the target. Should one movement end too soon or too late, you will diminish the power and precision of the action.

Internal timing is concerned with the fact that different parts of your body move at different speeds and through different distances. Good technique requires that you coordinate these speeds and distances.

In particular, we are concerned with coordinating the timing of the arms with that of the legs. Your arms can move the jo through the arc of a sweep or a strike faster than you can walk forward. If you begin to walk and sweep at the same time, the jo will hit the target before your forward foot is in position. To adjust your timing, you could slow your sweep so that the step and sweep begin and end at the same time. But that would reduce the power of the sweep. However, you can also start the motion of your arms later than your step, which will allow you to sweep with full power and end in time with the step.

You can train yourself to delay the sweep or strike by "cocking" the jo as you begin to step. Cock the jo simply by straightening your left arm slightly as you begin to sweep or strike. This will move the end of the jo backward a little, delaying the action of your arms a moment. If you begin to step as you cock, your foot will be in position just before the jo hits the target.

In the early stages of training, the cocking motion will be an obvious one. As you improve, you should substitute a slight tightening of the left hand for the straightening of the arm, which will produce the same delay without the backward movement of the jo. The delay appears in every strike or sweep accompanied by a full step. It is a subtle but important element of internal timing.

Practicing on a real target (a *makiwara*) will help develop a sense of internal timing because the point of impact can be seen and felt as you hit. Practicing without a makiwara is less effective because you cannot see or feel the point of impact, but it will teach you to focus mentally and physically on a point in space and to develop the control necessary to stop an action immediately after focusing it. A well-timed action should be stopped not by a counter-effort but by the position and resilience of your arms and body.

You may unconsciously compensate for a lack of timing in several ways. One way is to tense all your muscles and lock up just before impact. If you were to do this on a makiwara, your jo would bounce back sharply and you would feel the impact throughout your body. While your grip does tighten on impact, your body should be relaxed and assertive rather than tense and locked.

A second way to compensate for a lack of timing is by decelerating the jo during the last half of the action. This allows you to stop smoothly, but it eliminates the power of the action. On a makiwara, this would amount to lightly touching the target at the end of an otherwise strong action. The jo should accelerate during the action and hit the target with a maximum of force. If you are decelerating the jo, you may feel that you have control because you can stop it at the right time and place, but you do so at the expense of an effective action.

Still a third way to compensate for poor timing is by concentrating only on the moment of impact and forgetting about what happens after you hit the target. On a makiwara, this results in the jo bouncing off in random directions and usually means you made no attempt to stop the jo with control. There should be no follow-through with the jo as there is with a golf club or a baseball bat. Instead, focus the jo, stop it, and immediately move into another action.

Finally, timing can be lost unconsciously by moving from one action to another too soon. Be sure each action is precise and complete before moving to the next. If you move correctly, your movements will look crisp but connected. If you are moving from one action to another too soon, your movements will look fluid but will be without effective impact. Be especially careful when practicing alone, for it is easy to pay attention only to the continuity between your actions and to neglect the crispness that should mark every impact.

External Timing

External timing is concerned with the timing of your actions in relation to those of an opponent. Obviously, offensive and defensive actions must be timed to the openings and attacks of your opponent to be effective. In paired practice, external timing is readily apparent. Solo practice requires additional caution.

When practicing alone, it is easy to develop a rhythmic, waltz-like timing in which each action occurs at regular intervals. This is normal for most students and is adequate in the beginning of training.

Another aspect of timing in the techniques, however, is dictated by the actions as they occur in combat. For example, a common pattern is to follow an offensive action with a defensive one, such as following a thrust with a parry. If you were to perform this pattern with waltz-like timing, it would take as long to parry as to thrust. In reality, you must parry immediately after thrusting. This will destroy the waltz-like rhythm. In other words, your opponent often dictates the timing of your actions because you must respond to his. Thus, to develop external timing by yourself, you must know the hypothetical actions of your imagined opponent as well as the reasons for your own actions.

7. TRADITIONAL SHORT FORMS

In this section we present 22 short forms or *suburi* for the jo. Suburi teach the different ways of thrusting, striking, sweeping, and receiving. They are simple techniques that usually involve only one or two steps. Most of the suburi here are found in one or both kata or are similar to moves found in the kata. We have arranged them in five categories: thrusts, strikes, single-hand forms, outside figure-eight forms, and flowing forms. The suburi are numbered consecutively through the categories so you can refer to them quickly when they appear in the kata.

THRUSTS *Tsuki No Bu*

To thrust underhand from sankakutai, bend your rear knee to shift your weight to your rear leg. Lift the jo straight up with your left hand; your hand should come to about shoulder height (Fig. 61). Grip the shaft with your right hand at about waist level. Draw the jo forward with your left hand and let your right hand slide to the butt as you advance your forward foot—you should feel that you are stepping beside the jo—and bring your right arm back in preparation to thrust (Fig. 62). This will bring the jo to the horizontal. Thrust the jo forward with your right arm (Fig. 63), shift most of your weight to your forward knee, and slide your rear foot to the left of the reference line. Immediately after impact, slide your rear foot back across the reference line and bring the jo back and up over your head (Fig. 64). Slide your forward foot to the right of the reference line to take your body from the line of attack. Deflect your opponent's jo to your left with the end of your jo (Fig. 65). Keep your shoulders down, and shift most of your weight to your forward foot.

Suburi 1: *Choku Tsuki* (underhand front thrust) Figs. 61 through 65. From sankakukai (Fig. 61), thrust underhand to your opponent's chest (Fig. 63), then deflect his counter-thrust to your left (Fig. 65).

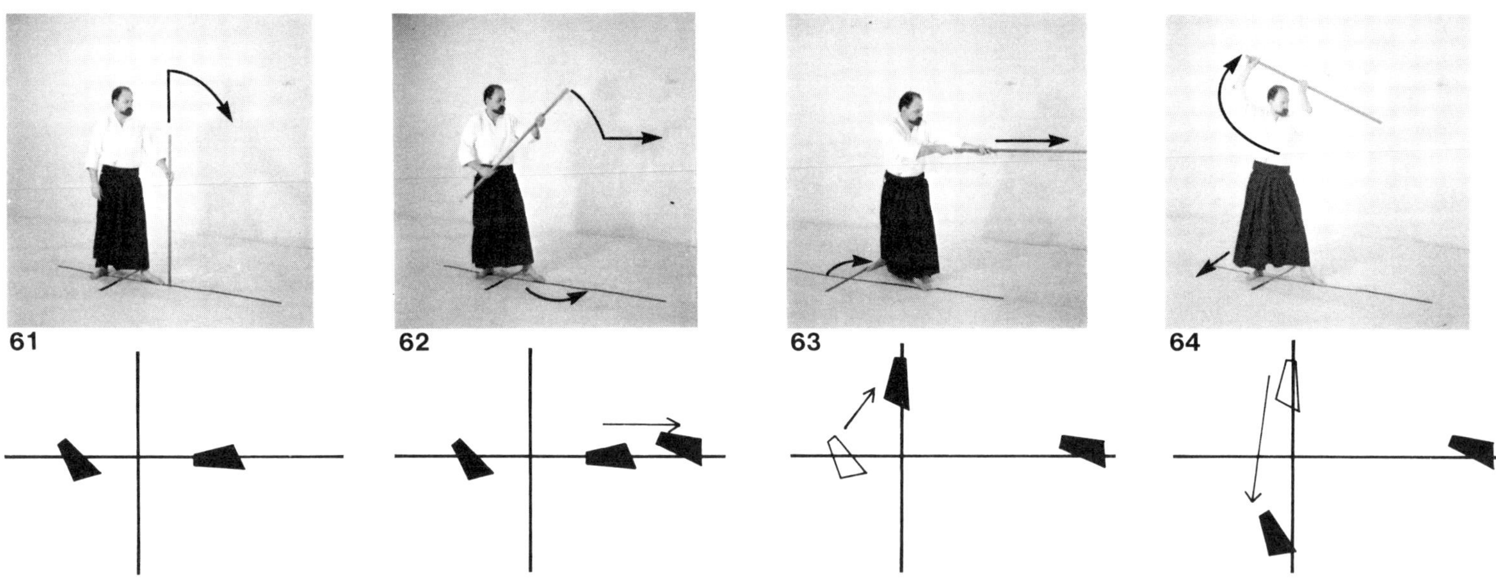

Suburi 2: *Tsuki Jodan Gaeshi* (front thrust, strike) Figs. 61 through 68. From sankakutai (Fig. 61), thrust underhand to your opponent's chest (Fig. 63), then deflect his counterthrust to the left (Fig. 65), hand-change (Fig. 66), and attack with a right yokomen strike (Fig. 68).

With a hand-change, you may continue suburi 1 into a right yokomen strike. Begin the hand-change immediately after the deflection (Fig. 66b) by sliding your right hand along the shaft to your left hand (Fig. 66c). Release your left hand and start the jo turning counterclockwise (Fig. 66d). Continue to turn the jo with your right hand and regrip the butt with your left hand as the jo comes around (Fig. 66e). As you complete the hand-change, step forward (Fig. 67) and attack with a right yokomen strike (Fig. 68).

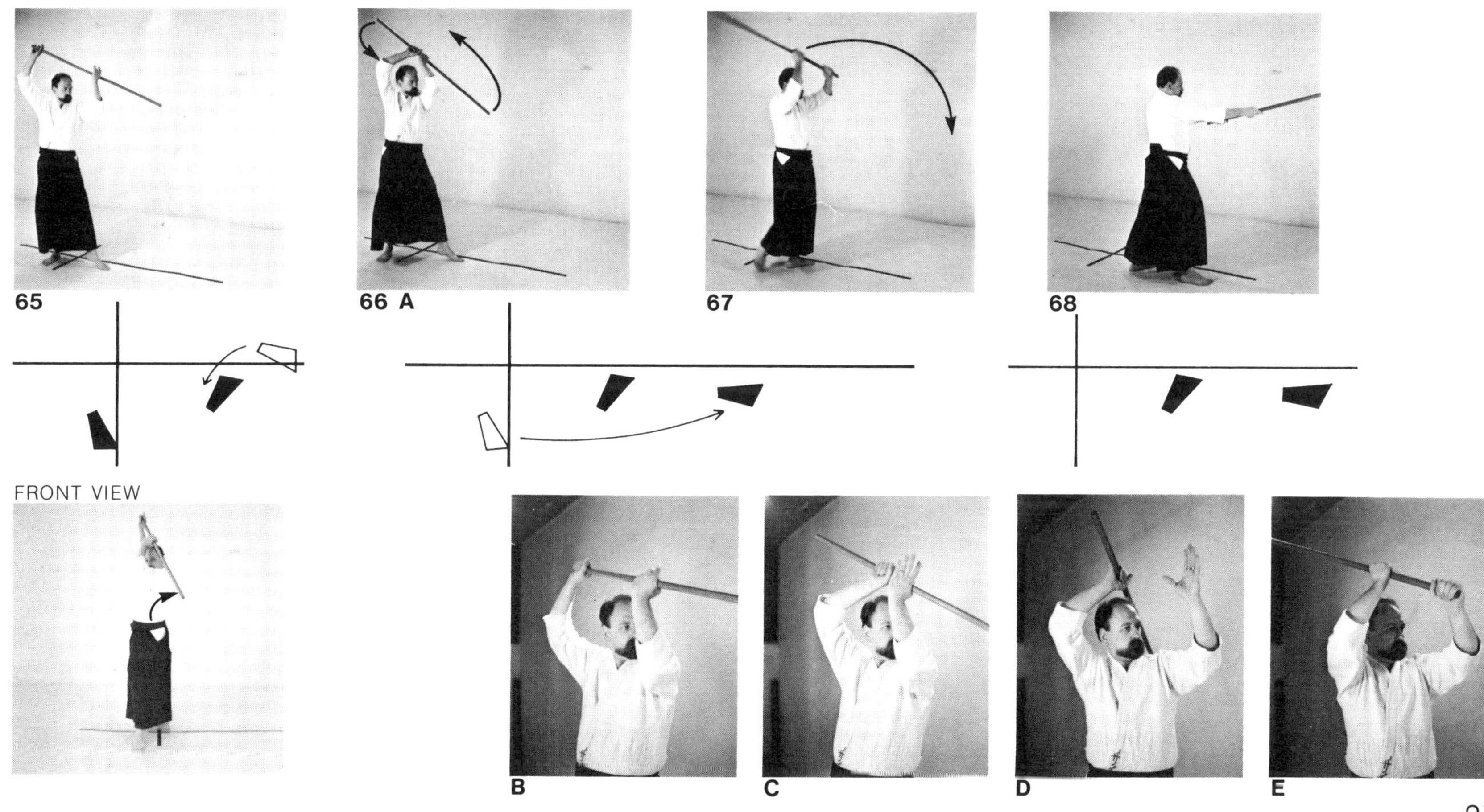

65 66 A 67 68

B C D E

To thrust overhand from sankakutai, bend your rear knee slightly to put weight on your rear foot. Grip the butt of the jo with your right hand, thumb down (Fig. 70). Bring your right hand back to your hip. This will circle the jo to the outside and up to the horizontal. Advance your forward foot at the same time. You should feel that you are stepping beside the jo. Thrust the jo forward with your right arm (Fig. 72) and slide your back foot to the left of the reference line.

At the end of the thrust, slide your back foot across the reference line and bring the jo up (Fig. 73). Slide your forward foot forcefully to the right of the reference line and push your opponent's jo to your right with the end of your jo (Fig. 74). Keep your left hand stationary and move your right hand up and over

Suburi 3: *Kaeshi Tsuki* (overhand front thrust) Figs. 69 through 74. From sankakutai (Fig. 69), thrust overhand to your opponent's chest (Fig. 72), then deflect his counterthrust to your right (Fig. 74).

69

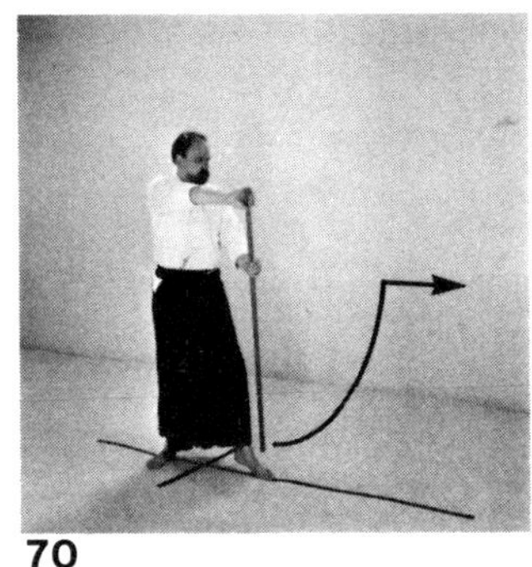

70

71

your head. This produces a hooking motion at the end of your jo that deflects your opponent's thrust. Avoid pushing your jo into the deflection with your left hand.

In suburi 1, you deflected his jo to your left and moved to the right of the line of attack. This does not take much force because you are simply protecting yourself as you move out of the line of attack. In suburi 3, you are deflecting his jo to your right and are moving to the right yourself. This means that instead of avoiding his jo, you are forcefully moving it from the line of attack. To do this, your steps to the right must be strong and you must use your right hand to power the deflection.

The steps in suburi 3 are the same as those in suburi 1.

72

73

74 A

B

Suburi 4: *Tsuki Gedan Gaeshi* (front thrust, sweep) Figs. 69 through 72 and 75 through 78. From sankakutai (Fig. 69), thrust overhand to your opponent's chest (Fig. 72), withdraw (Fig. 75), and attack with an advancing overhand sweep (Fig. 78).

Suburi 3 may be ended with a sweep by replacing the deflection with a hand-change. At the end of the thrust (Fig. 72), slide your back foot across the reference line and withdraw the jo through your left hand (Fig. 75). Thrust the jo to the rear through your right hand with your left and slide your forward foot to the right of the reference line (Fig. 76). Step forward (Fig. 77) and attack with an overhand sweep (Fig. 78).

The steps in suburi 4 are the same as those in suburi 2.

69

70

71

72

75

76

77

78

Suburi 5: *Ushiro Tsuki Dai Ipon* (underhand rear thrust) Figs. 79 through 82. From sankakutai (Fig. 79), thrust underhand to an opponent at your right rear (Fig.82).

Begin as in the underhand front thrust, but shift your weight to your forward foot. Take a small step back with your back foot, look back to your right, and thrust to the knee of an opponent behind you.

79

80

81

82

Suburi 6: *Ushiro Tsuki Dai Nipon* (overhand rear thrust) Figs. 83 through 86. From sankakutai (Fig. 83), thrust overhand to the knee of an opponent at your left rear (Fig. 86).

Begin as in an overhand front thrust, but instead of circling the jo forward to the horizontal, look back to your left, step back with your left foot, and thrust to the knee of an opponent behind you. Let your left shin hide the jo from your opponent as long as possible during the step (Fig. 85b).

83

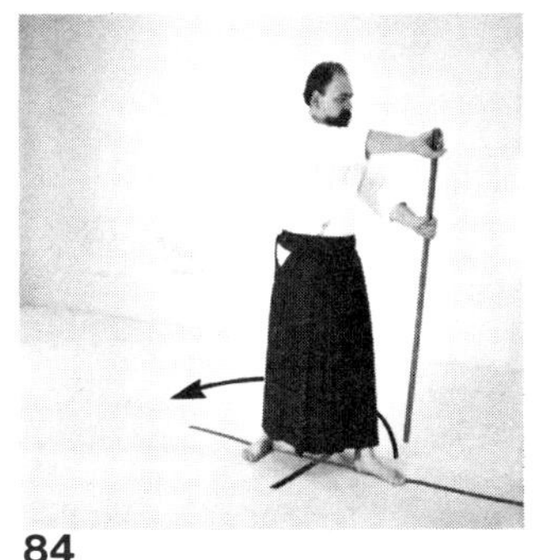
84

85

86

FRONT VIEW

Strikes *Uchikomi No Bu*

Suburi 7: *Shomen Uchi* (vertical strike) Figs. 87 through 91. From chudan (Fig. 87), retreat to jodan (Fig. 88), then attack with a vertical strike (Fig. 91).

To retreat from chudan to jodan, bend your back knee to take weight from your front foot, step back, and push your jo up. Think of pushing yourself down, underneath the jo, as you step. In jodan for the shomen strike (Fig. 88b), look at your opponent from under your left elbow, step forward, and strike straight down. Turn your shoulders to the left as you strike. Keep your left knee flexed to prevent floating during the two steps with your right foot. Cock the jo as you begin to step and before you strike to time the step with the strike.

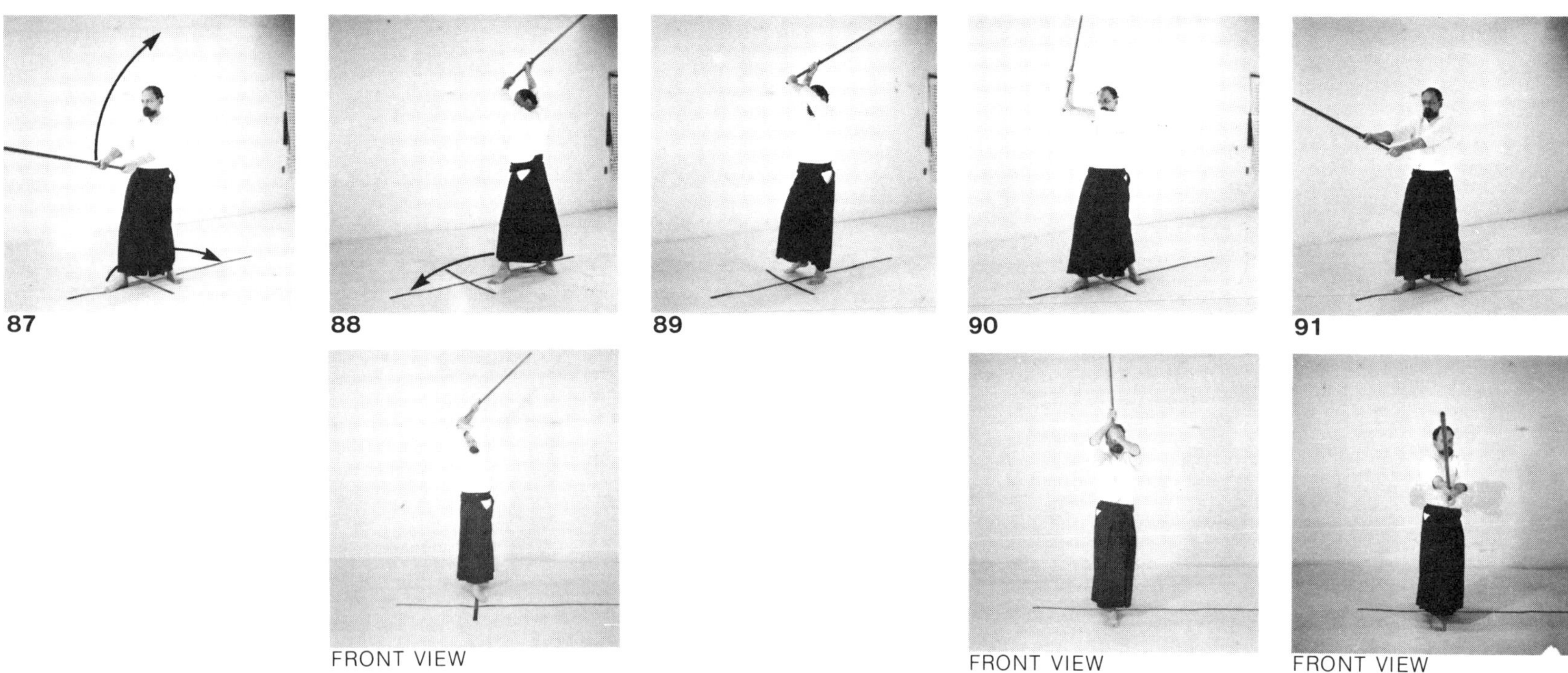

87

88

89

90

91

FRONT VIEW

FRONT VIEW

FRONT VIEW

Suburi 8: *Yokomen Uchi* (diagonal strike) Figs. 92 through 96. From chudan (Fig. 92), retreat to jodan (Fig. 93), then attack with a right yokomen strike (Fig. 96).

Retreat to jodan as in suburi 7. In jodan for the yokomen strike, look at your opponent over your left arm (Fig. 93b). Step forward with your right foot and strike at an angle. Aside from the angle of the strike and the variation of the jodan posture, this suburi is the same as suburi 7.

92 93 94 95 96

FRONT VIEW FRONT VIEW FRONT VIEW

Suburi 9: *Renzoku* (consecutive strikes) Figs. 92 through 104. From chudan (Fig. 92), retreat to jodan (Fig. 93), then attack with a right yokomen strike (Fig. 96), a left yokomen strike (Fig. 101), and a right yokomen strike (Fig. 104).

Continue suburi 8 by lifting the butt with your left hand, rolling the jo around to your right, and walking forward into a left yokomen strike (Fig. 101). Continue walking forward as you lift and roll the jo back around into a right yokomen strike (Fig. 104). Always lift the jo with your left hand during the rolls.

This suburi moves you from a right stance to a left one, and back again. It also prepares you for actions involving movement to the sides. The rolling motions can also be used as blocks.

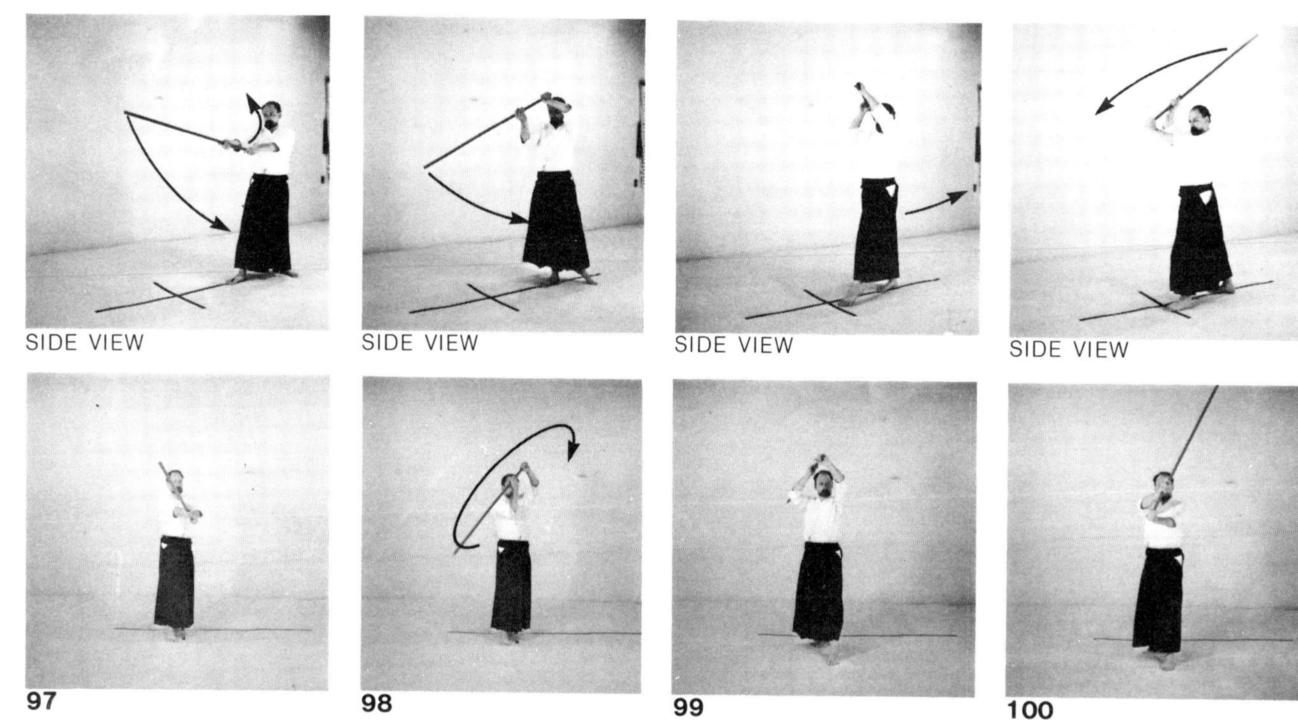

SIDE VIEW SIDE VIEW SIDE VIEW SIDE VIEW

97 98 99 100

SIDE VIEW SIDE VIEW SIDE VIEW SIDE VIEW

101 102 103 104

Suburi 10: *Menuchi Gedan Gaeshi* (strike and sweep) Figs. 105 through 112. From chudan (Fig. 105), retreat to jodan (Fig. 106), attack with a yokomen strike (Fig. 107), hand-change, and attack with a reverse-hand sweep (Fig. 112).

Suburi 10 combines a right yokomen strike (suburi 8) with a sliding hand-change and a left sweep (as in suburi 4). Take a small step back with your left foot as you withdraw the jo during the hand-change (Fig. 108). Let your right foot slide back a little before you begin to sweep (Fig. 109).

105

106

107

108

109

110

111

112

From chudan, roll into a left yokomen strike with the motions of suburi 9. You will move from a right to a left stance. Perform the hand-change (Figs. 116 and 117) by releasing your left hand and extending it forward along the shaft while drawing the jo back with your right hand. When your left hand reaches the end (Fig. 117), tighten your grip and thrust to the rear (Fig. 118) as in suburi 5.

Suburi 11: *Yokomen Ushiro Tsuki Dai Ipon* (strike and thrust) Figs. 113 through 118. From chudan (Fig. 113), attack with a left yokomen strike (Fig. 116), then thrust to an opponent at your right rear (Fig. 118).

113

114

115

116

117

118

Single-Hand Forms *(Katate No Bu)*

Withdraw from an underhand front thrust by pushing your jo to the rear through your right hand as you slide your back foot across the reference line. Let your forward foot slide back a little, then step forward with your back foot and swing the jo vertically past your right side. When the jo passes your right knee, turn your right hand to the outside to bring the jo up in front of you to the horizontal, where the beat occurs (Fig. 124). Support the jo with your left hand at the top of the beat to help control the swing. You may continue your movement by sliding into the right yokomen strike, a thrust, or a jab.

Suburi 12: *Katate Gedan Gaeshi* (upward beat) Figs. 119 through 125. From sankakutai (Fig. 119), thrust underhand (Fig. 120), withdraw (Fig. 121), then counter your opponent's thrust by beating his jo up and away (Fig. 125).

119

120

121

122

123

124

125

This suburi allows you to strike an opponent who would otherwise be out of range. From a front thrust, withdraw your jo over your head (Fig. 128), then step forward with your right foot as you swing your extended right arm around, holding the jo. Strike your opponent's head. Keep your left arm extended toward him. You may let the jo swing all the way around to the left side or, after it strikes, withdraw it in preparation for a thrust.

Suburi 13: *Toma Katate Uchi* (distance strike) Figs. 126 through 132. From sankakutai (Fig. 126), thrust underhand (Fig. 127), withdraw (Fig. 128), then swing your jo horizontally at your opponent's head (Fig. 132).

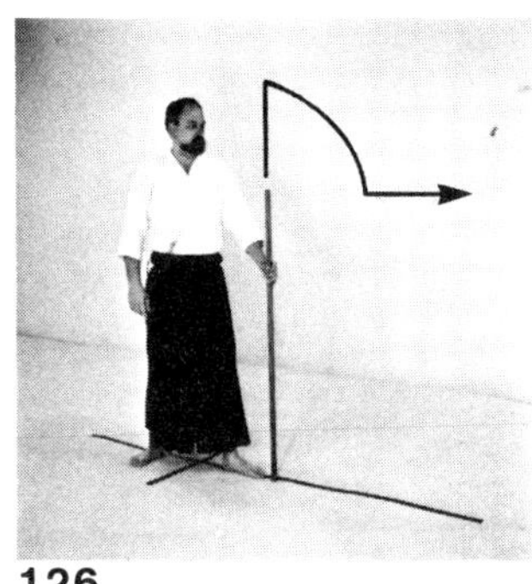

126

127

128

129

130

131

132

This suburi translates roughly as "one-hand outside figure eight." The fact that the motion can be described in English as a "horizontal figure eight" is only coincidence. The Japanese character for the number eight consists of two diagonal lines resembling an inverted V. The lines represent the down strokes of the jo as they cross in front of you.

Begin the hand-change after an overhand front thrust (Fig. 134) by releasing your right hand. Let the end drop and swing down, past your right side. Regrip with your right hand below your left as the jo becomes horizontal (Fig. 135). Step back with your left foot at the same time. Release your left hand and begin swinging the jo in a horizontal figure eight (Figs. 136 through 138).

The forestalling action may be continued as long as necessary. It may be done while walking forward or backward, although you should time your steps to avoid hitting your knees. You may receive your opponent's jo by hooking it

133

134

135

136

137

Suburi 14: *Katate Hachi No Ji Gaeshi* (Figs. 133 through 142). From sankakutai (Fig. 133), thrust overhand (Fig. 134), hand-change (Fig. 135), then forestall your opponent by swinging your jo rapidly from side to side in a horitontal figure eight pattern (Figs. 136 through 138), and withdraw into hasso no kamae (Fig. 142).

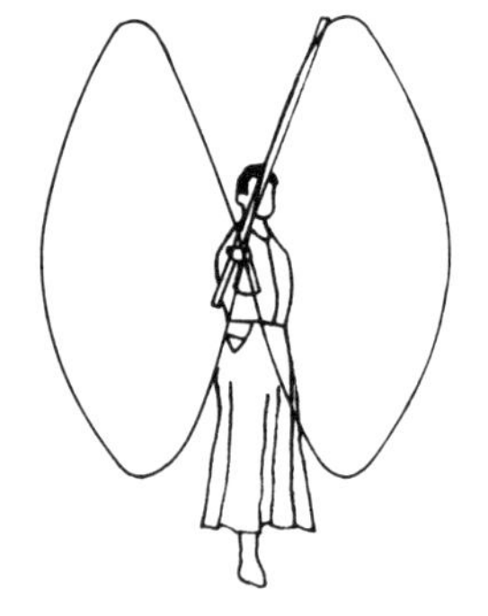

with the short end of your jo (Fig. 136) and you may use the down stroke as a one-hand, back-hand beat (Fig. 137), or as a backhand strike (Fig. 138).

To come out of the figure eight, step back with your right foot as you swing the jo down past your right side (Fig. 139). When the jo becomes vertical, grip the butt with your left hand, thumb down, and swing the jo up to your shoulder as in hasso no kamae (Fig. 142). (Your right hand will be thumb-down, rather than thumb-up as in hasso no kamae.)

138

139

140

141

142

Outside Figure Eight Forms *(Hasso Gaeshi No Bu)*

Hasso No Kamae Preparation

Figs. 143 through 150.

Suburi 15 through 18 begin by moving from chudan to hasso no kamae. To move into hasso no kamae, withdraw the jo through your right hand (Fig. 144), and step back with your right foot. With your left hand, throw the butt of the jo out and down so it will come up past your right side (Fig. 146). The movement may be used to beat aside an opponent's jo. Regrip the jo with your left hand, thumb down, as the jo comes *down* to the vertical (Fig. 147). As the jo comes *up*

143

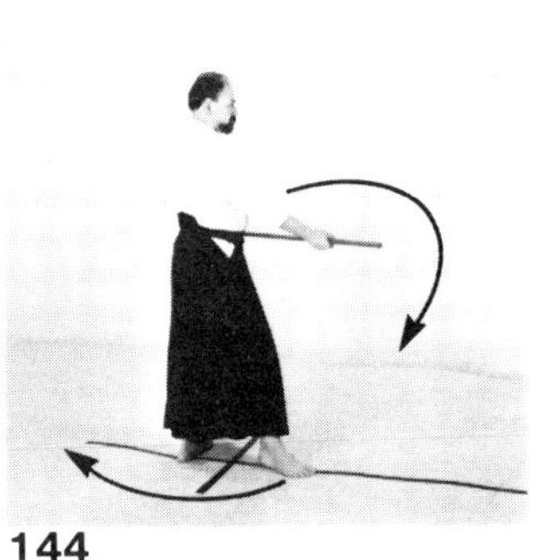
144

145

146

to the vertical, pivot the base of your right palm on the shaft (Fig. 149) and roll your hand around the jo before regripping. Your right hand should be thumb-up. In each hasso no bu suburi, establish the hasso no kamae posture (Fig. 150)—but only for an instant—before continuing the suburi.

SIDE VIEW

SIDE VIEW

147

148

149

150

Suburi 15: *Hasso Gaeshi Tsuki* (reverse hand thrust) Figs. 143 through 154. From chudan (Fig. 143), move to hasso no kamae (Fig. 151), then deliver a reverse-hand thrust to your opponent's face (Fig. 154).

From hasso no kamae (Fig. 151), draw the jo through your right hand with the left and advance your forward foot. Thrust as your forward knee accepts weight. For a straighter thrust, think of pushing your right hand to the left along the jo, rather than trying to guide the end to the target.

143

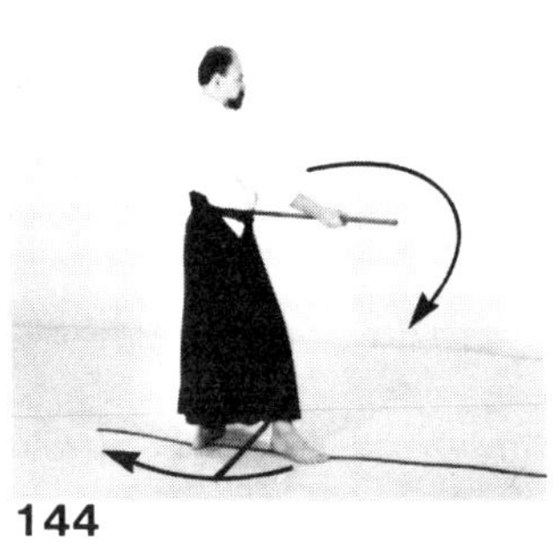
144

145

146

151

152

147 148 149 150
153 154

Suburi 16: *Hasso Gaeshi Uchi* (front strike) Figs. 143 through 151 and 155 through 157. From chudan (Fig. 143), move to hasso no kamae (Fig. 151), then attack with a right yokomen strike Fig. 157).

Walk forward with your right foot as you strike. Remember to cock the jo as you begin to step to adjust your timing.

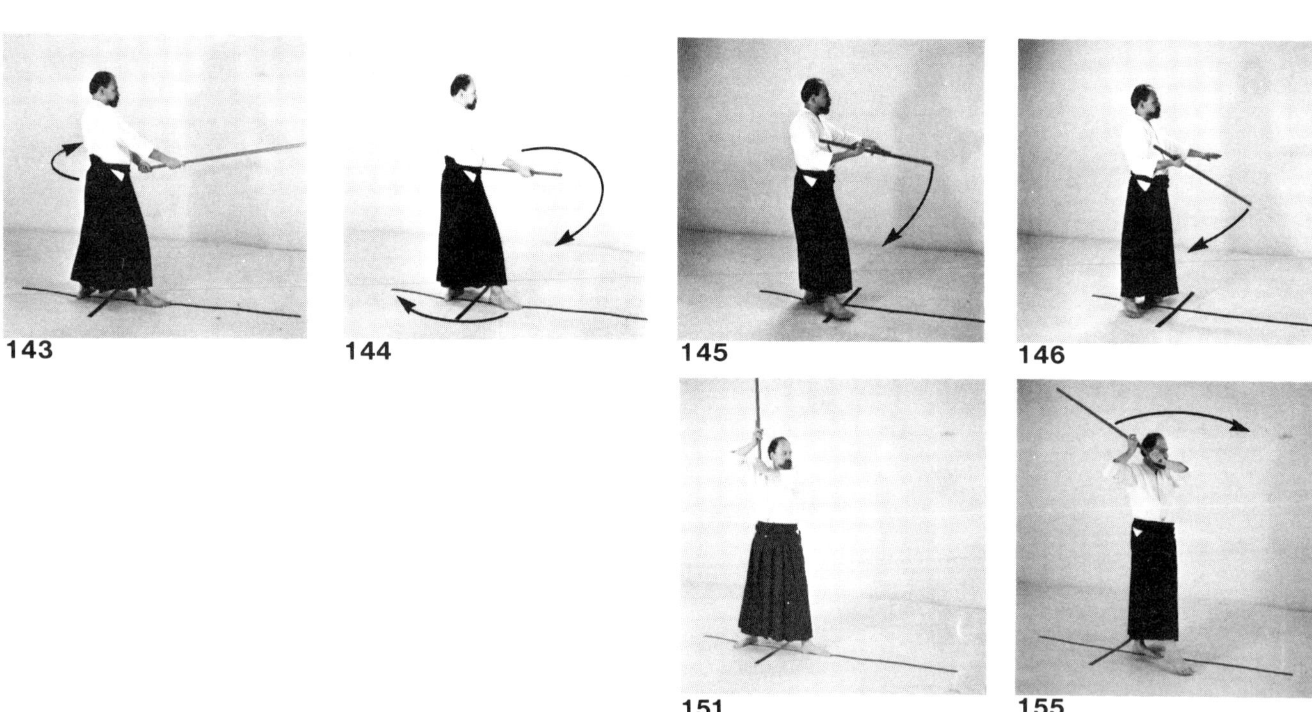

143 144 145 146 151 155

147 148 149 150

156 157

Suburi 17: *Hasso Gaeshi Ushiro Uchi* (rear strike) Figs. 143 through 150 and 158 through 160. From chudan (Fig. 143), move to hasso no kamae (Fig. 158), then pivot and attack an opponent behind you with a shomen strike (Fig. 160).

From hasso no kamae, pivot 180 degrees to your right and deliver a shomen strike.

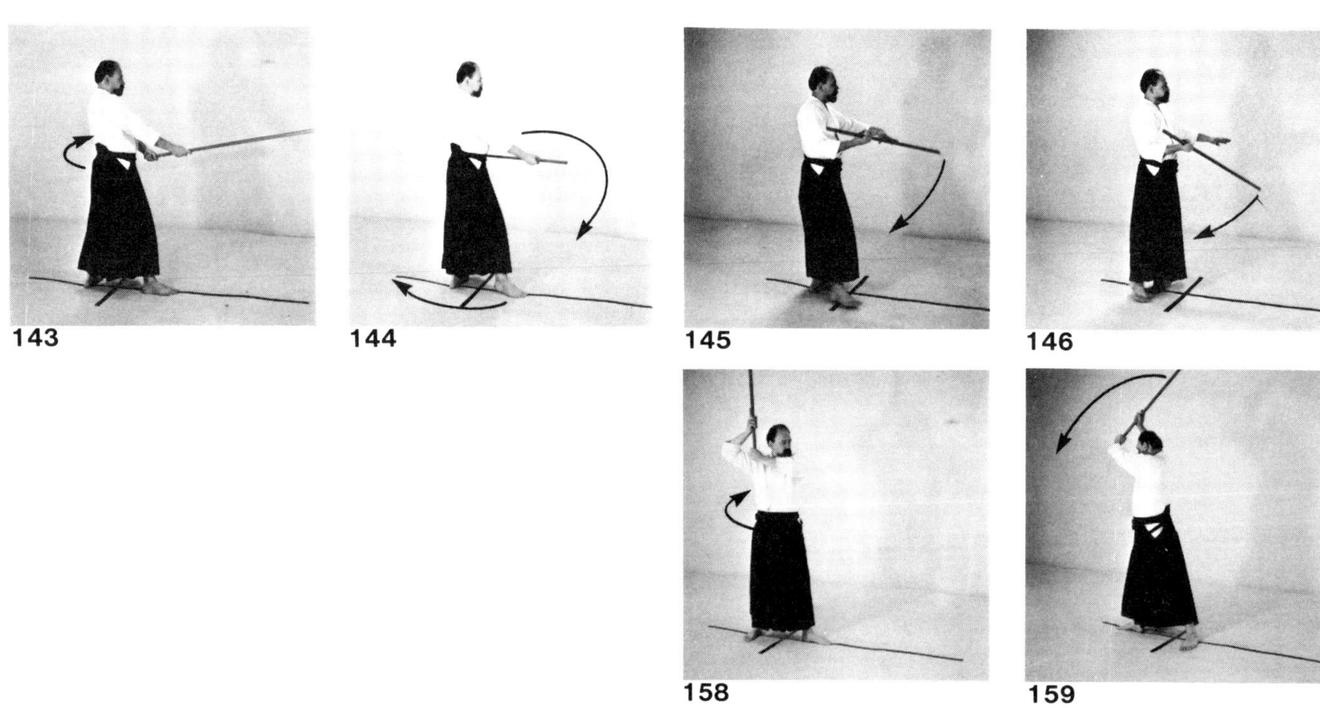

143 144 145 146

158 159

147

148

149

150

160

Suburi 18: *Hasso Gaeshi Ushiro Harai* (beating rear strike) Figs. 143 through 150 and 158 through 163. From chudan (Fig. 143), move to hasso no kamae (Fig. 158), then counter a thrust to your back by beating your opponent's jo down and away (Fig. 161).

From hasso no kamae, pivot 180 degrees to your right, then step back with your right foot and swing your jo in a downward spiral to your right. You are striking your opponent's jo from above and are beating it down and to the right (Fig. 161). End in the waka no kamae posture (Fig. 163).

143 144 145 146

158 159 160

147 148 149 150

161 162 163

Flowing Forms *(Nagare Gaeshi No Bu)*

Suburi 19: *Gyaku Yokomen Ushiro Tuski Dai Nipon* (strike and rear thrust) Figs. 164 through 171. From chudan (Fig. 164), attack with a left yokomen strike (Fig. 167), hand-change, deflect your opponent's thrust (Fig. 168), then hand-change again and thrust to your left rear (Fig. 171).

The hand-change is similar to that in suburi 11, but more retiring. Immediately after the left yokomen strike, release your left hand and draw the jo back and up into the deflection with your right as in suburi 1. As your right hand passes over your left, bring your left hand up and support the jo. When the jo is in position, tighten your grip (Fig. 168). In this hand-change, your left hand does not extend but rather lifts. Use the end of the jo to deflect a thrust to your left, or use the shaft (the area between your hands) to receive a strike. Immediately after receiving his jo, throw the butt of your jo forward, out, and down with your right hand to

164

165

166

167

push his jo out of the way. At the same time, step back with your left foot (Fig. 169), regrip with your right hand, palm up, and thrust underhand to your left rear (Fig. 171).

168

169

170

171

Suburi 20: *Hasso Gaeshi Ushiro Tsuki* (flowing rear thrust) Figs. 172 through 180. From chudan (Fig. 172), move to hasso no kamae (Fig. 177), then hand-change and thrust to an opponent at your right rear (Fig. 180).

Move from hasso no kamae (Figs. 172 to 177) by pivoting 180 degrees to your right. Release your left hand, and draw the jo out toward your opponent with your right hand (Fig. 178). Regrip with your left hand and thrust overhand. The suburi should be one continuous motion. Keep your weight centered between your knees during the pivot.

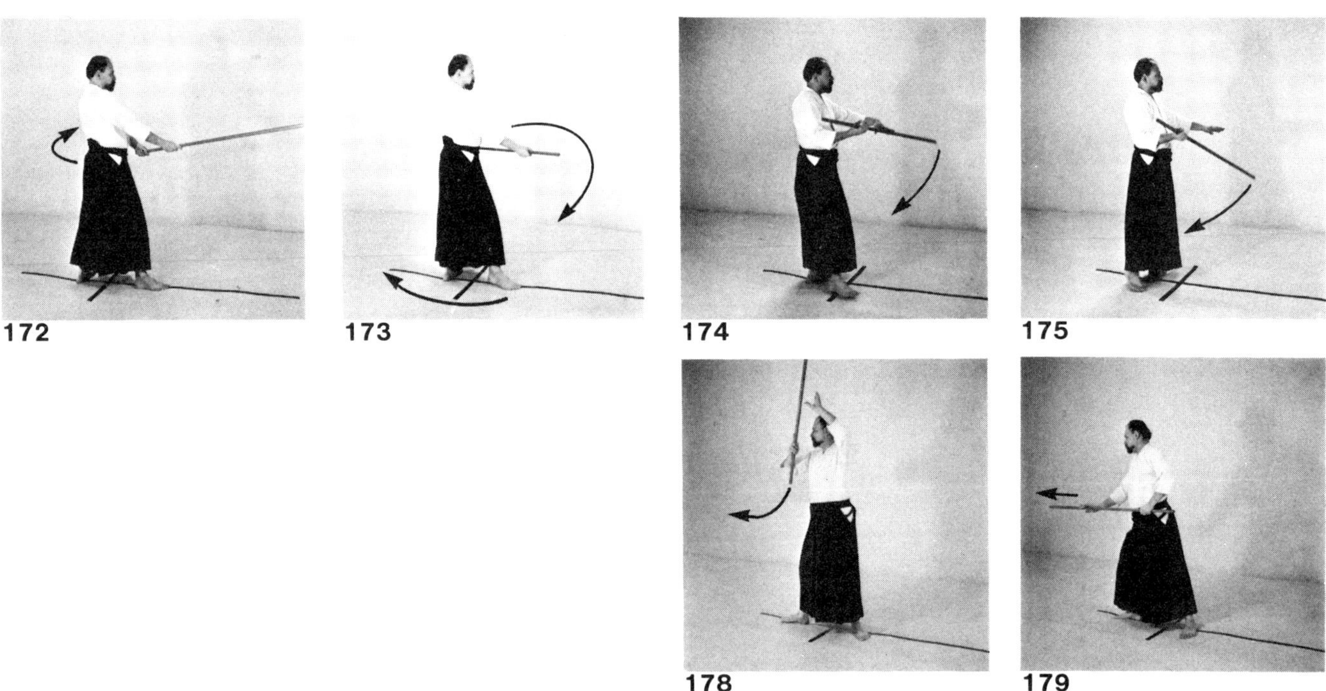

172 173 174 175 178 179

176

177

180

The first hand-change and the turn in this suburi take you from suburi 8 to suburi 2. Complete a right yokomen strike as in suburi 8, then pivot 180 degrees to your left and release your left hand. Lift your right elbow to begin your pivot. Pass the butt underneath your right forearm and turn your right hand over to bring the jo up for deflection. Regrip with your left hand, palm up, and deflect your opponent's jo. Hand-change, and deliver a second yokomen strike as in suburi 2. Be careful to focus the first strike before moving into the deflection.

Suburi 21: *Hidari Nagare Gaeshi Uchi* (left flowing strike) Figs. 181 through 189. From chudan (Fig. 181), retreat to jodan (Fig. 182), then attack with a right yokomen strike (Fig. 183). Continue the strike into a pivot (Fig. 184) and deflect a thrust to your back (Fig. 186). Hand-change (Fig. 187), and attack with a right yokomen strike (Fig. 189).

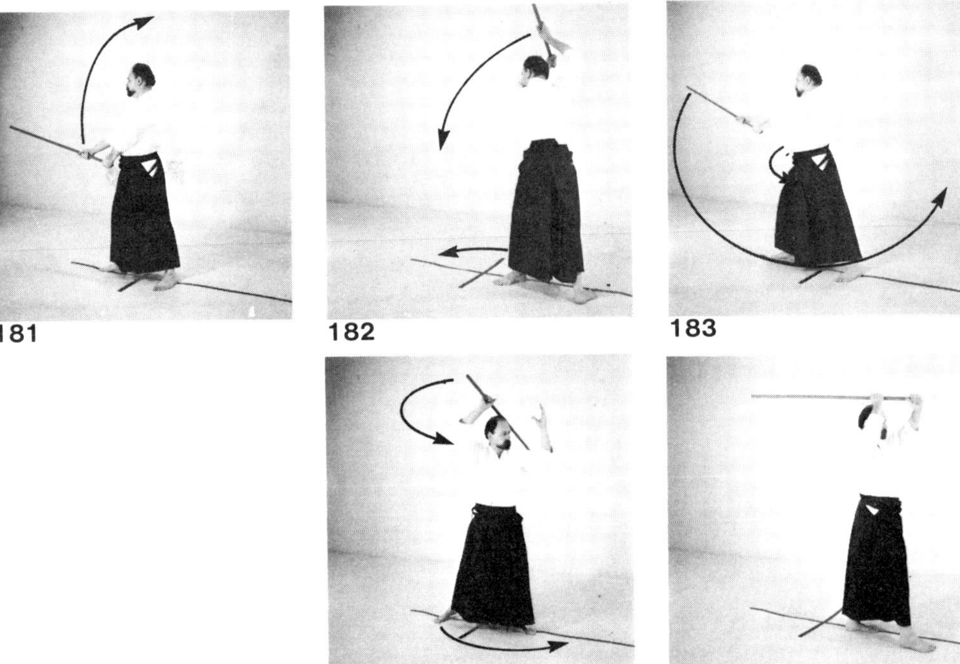

181 182 183

187 188

185

186

Suburi 22: *Migi Nagare Gaeshi Tsuki* (right flowing thrust) Figs. 190 through 197. From chudan (Fig. 190), attack with a left yokomen strike (Fig. 192). With a back step (Fig. 194), pivot 180 degrees to deflect a thrust at your back (Fig. 195), then thrust underhand (Fig. 197).

After the left yokomen strike (Fig. 192), shift your weight to your forward foot and bring your back foot around behind you to turn 180 degrees to the right (Fig. 194). Release your left hand from the butt as you begin to turn. Regrip the shaft with your left hand, palm up, and push the jo up into the deflection as you complete the pivot (Fig. 195). Roll out of the deflection and thrust underhand (Fig. 197). As in suburi 21, focus the strike before moving into the hand-change and deflection.

Take the time to experiment with these 22 suburi. Explore their possibilities and limitations; their similarities and differences. If your movements do not feel right, do something different: vary the position of your feet, hands, and shoulders at different points in the movement. Especially be aware of the motions of your elbows and knees. Do something wrong intentionally to see what happens—exaggerating your mistakes sometimes helps to identify them. Become familiar with the suburi so that you can combine them into your own forms. Practice turning to the sides and to the rear. Vary your strikes, thrusts, sweeps, and receiving actions. In this way, the subtleties of the jo will emerge, and you will appreciate the art more and more.

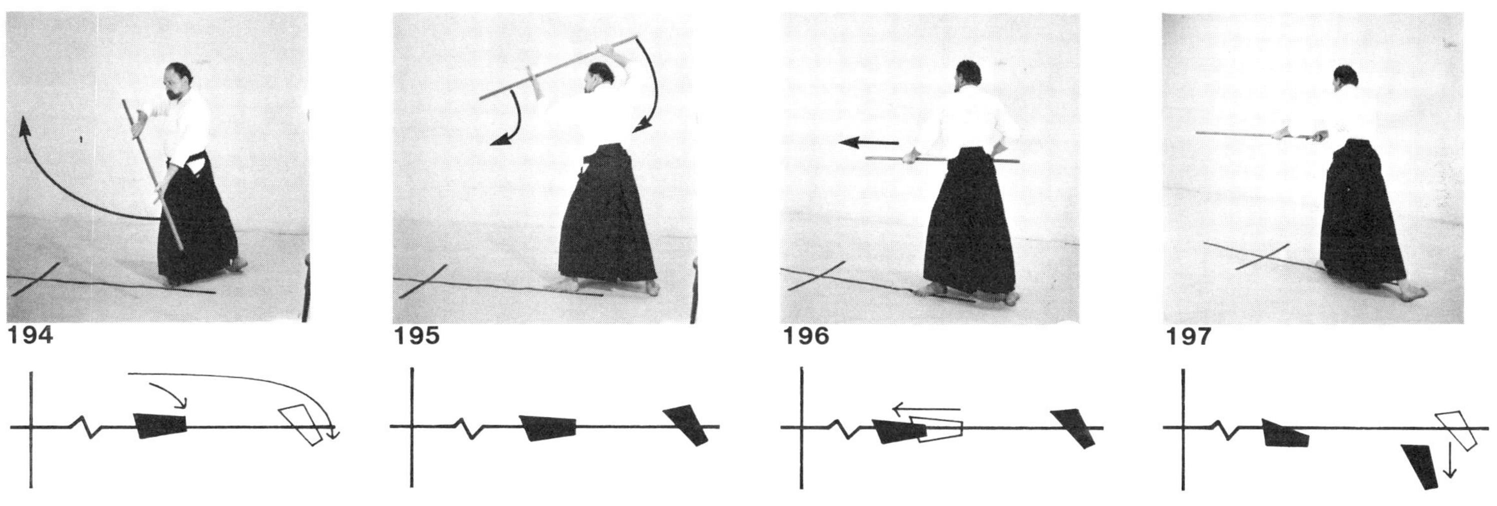
194
195
196
197

8. A MODERN PRACTICE FORM

The practice form shown in Figs. 198 through 217 involves right- and left-handed thrusts, strikes, and sweeps. It introduces the section on kata by showing how suburi can be blended into continuous movement.

The form is really two forms that may be practiced separately or together. In the first, you begin from chudan and roll into a left yokomen strike (Fig. 198), advance with a right reverse-hand sweep (Fig. 201), and end with a right front thrust (Fig. 203). Rolling into a left yokomen strike allows you to repeat the form. To move to the second form, simply hand-change and roll from a left yokomen strike into a right one (Fig. 208). Follow the strike with a left sweep (Fig. 211) and a right thrust (Fig. 213). Rolling into a deflection and a right yokomen strike (Fig. 214) allows you to repeat the form. To move from one form to the other, simply change at the strike. That is, roll from a left strike into a right one to move from the first form to the second. Roll from a strike into a left one to move back.

Practice slowly. Pay attention to your balance, precision, and smoothness.

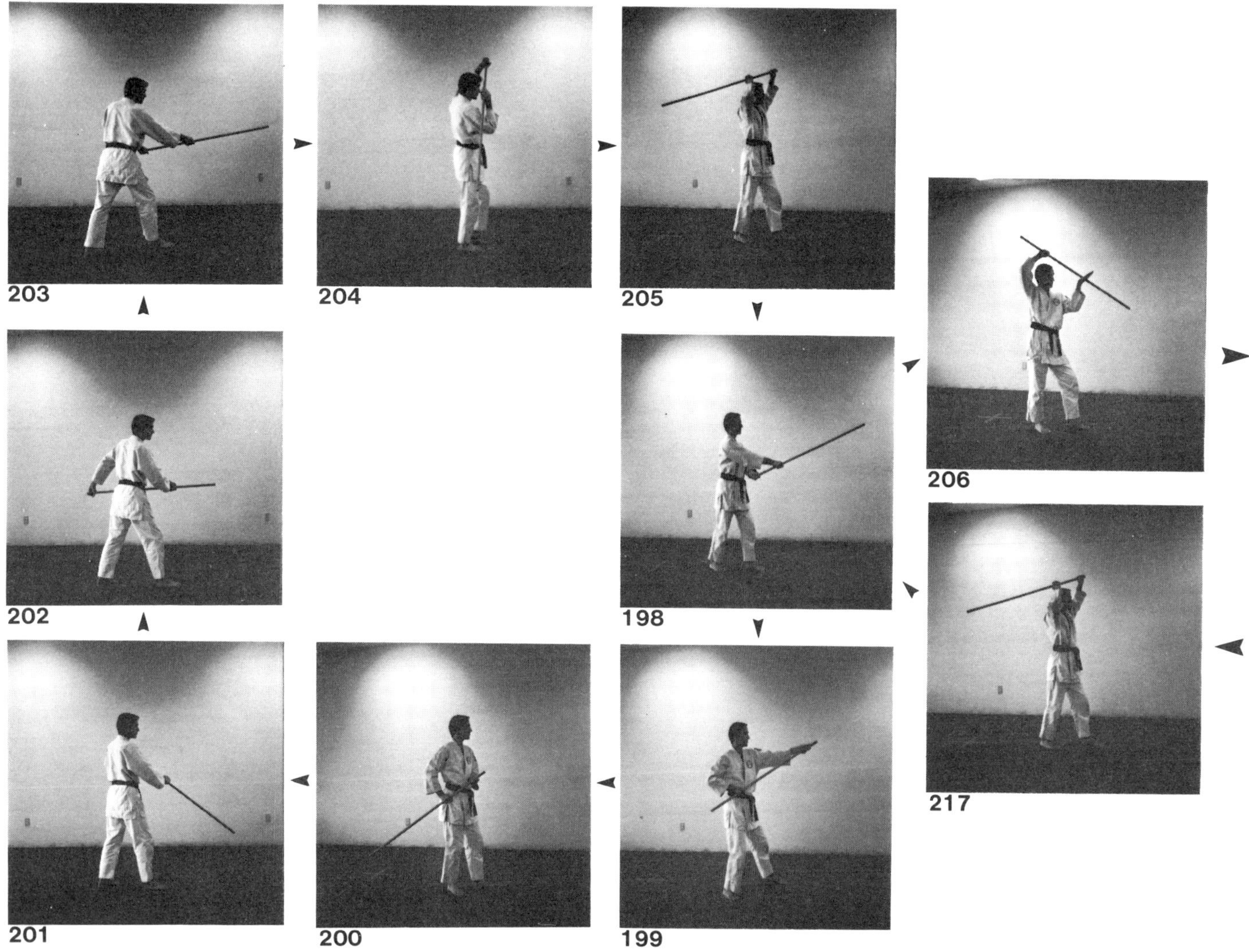
203
204
205
206
202
198
217
201
200
199

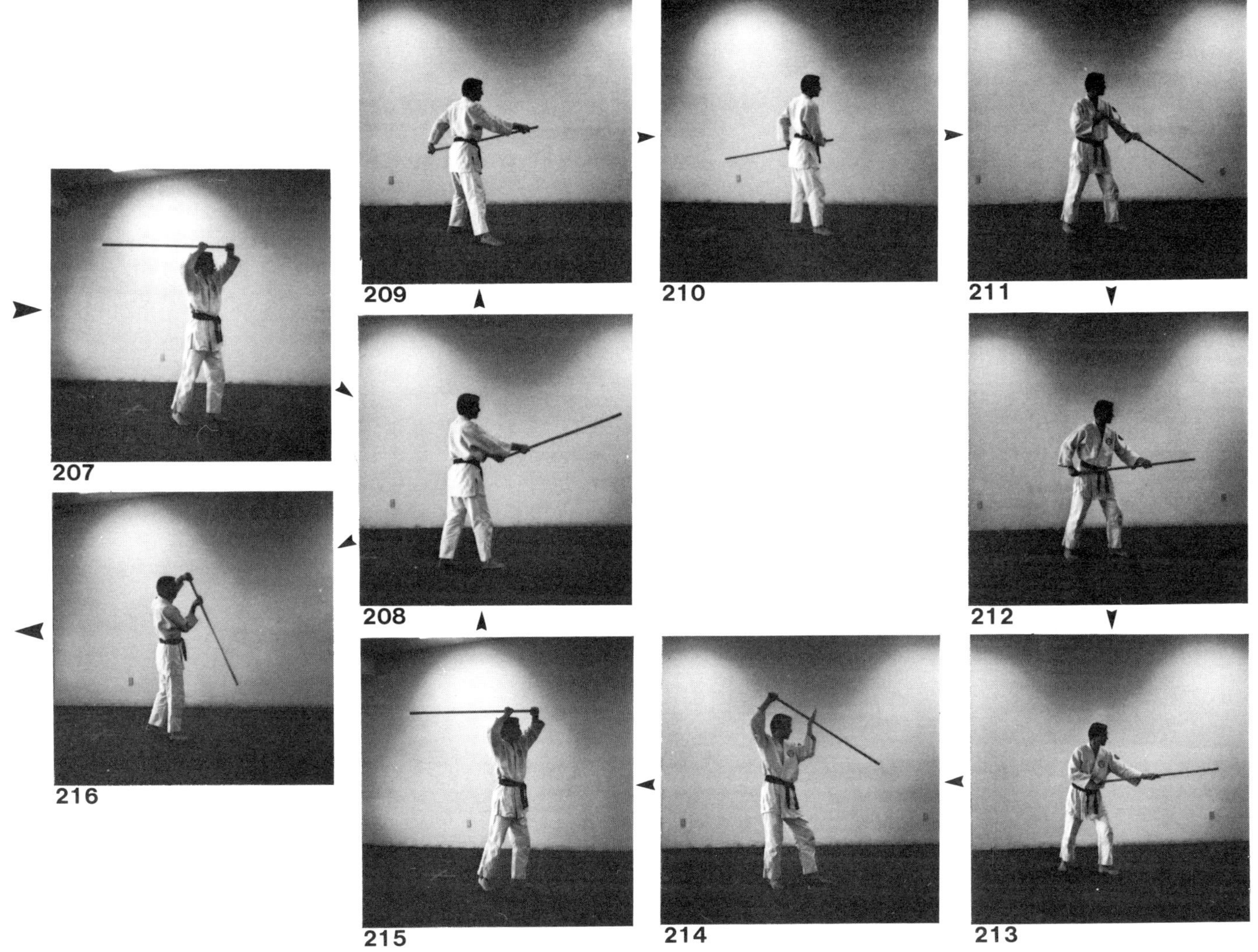
207 208 209 210 211 212 213 214 215 216

9. TRADITIONAL LONG FORMS

In this section we present two traditional long forms, or *kata,* for the short staff. Kata teach you how to move efficiently from one action to another and are intended to train you in movement. They are not necessarily simulated combat.

The kata we present here are referred to as *kata no nijuni* (the 22-count kata) and *kata no sanjuichi* (the 31-count kata). We chose these because they are the kata most commonly taught in the United States today. The counts are simply reference points that can aid in learning and teaching the form. In our presentation here, each count is numbered below the figure in which it occurs. Below each figure is also a brief title that identifies the movement in the figure. Suburi from the previous sections that appear in the kata are identified. Additional information and directions are in the figure captions.

Fig. 218 Begin in sankakutai.

Fig. 219 Thrust underhand to your opponent's chest and . . .

1

Fig. 220 Quickly deflect a counter-thrust by pushing it to your left.

Fig. 221 Drop out of the deflection and again thrust underhand to his chest.

Kata No Nijuni

2

Fig. 222 Parry another counter-thrust to your left and roll into a hand-change.

Fig. 223 Begin to advance with your right foot as you complete the hand-change and . . .

3

Fig. 224 Execute a right yokomen strike.

Fig. 225 Roll the jo around and . . .

4

Fig. 226 Attack with a left yokomen strike.

Fig. 227 Change the position of your left hand and . . .

5

Fig. 228 Thrust behind yourself at a second opponent's knee.

Fig. 229 Draw the jo out, pivot 180 degrees to your right, and . . .

FRONT VIEW

Fig. 230 Deflect his jo down and to your right.

6

Fig. 231 Walk forward with your left foot and thrust underhand to his chest.

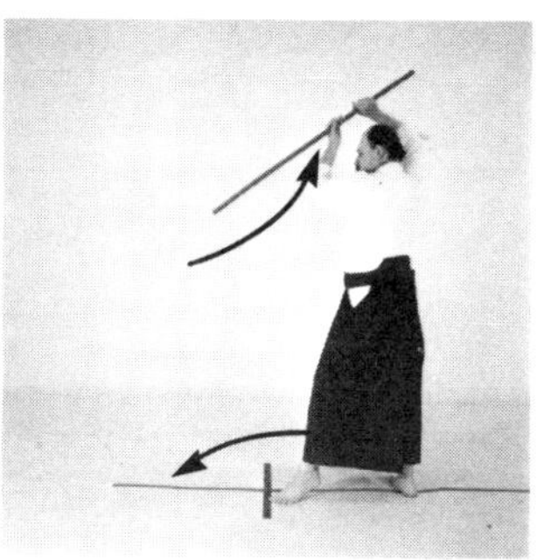

Fig. 232 Parry his counterthrust and. . . and . . .

7

Fig. 233 Roll into a right yokomen strike.

Fig. 234 Walk forward with your left foot and roll into . . .

8

Fig. 235 A left yokomen strike.

Fig. 236 Pivot 180 degrees to your right while maintaining the chudan posture and . . .

9

Fig. 237 Knock his jo out of your line of attack. (This is a *harai,* or a beating strike.)

10

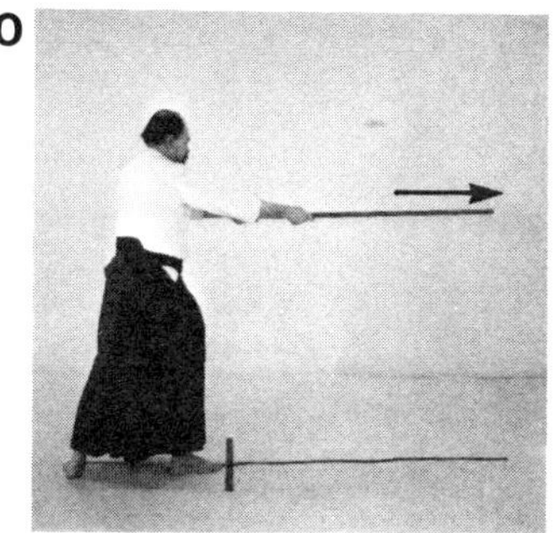

Fig. 238 Jab at his chest and . . .

Fig. 239 Roll into . . .

11

Fig. 240 A left yokomen strike.

12

Fig. 241 Change the position of your left hand and deflect his jo to your left.

Fig. 242 Throw your jo out and over with your right hand to throw his jo off.

Fig. 243 Regrip and . . .

13

Fig. 244 Thrust to the rear.

14

Fig. 245 Then thrust backhand at his face.

Fig. 246 Release your right hand, let the end drop, and . . .

Fig. 247 Turn the jo end-over-end.

15

Fig. 248 Thrust underhand to his chest and . . .

Fig. 249 Withdraw into a deflection. Throw your jo out and over with your right hand, regrip, and drop into . . .

16

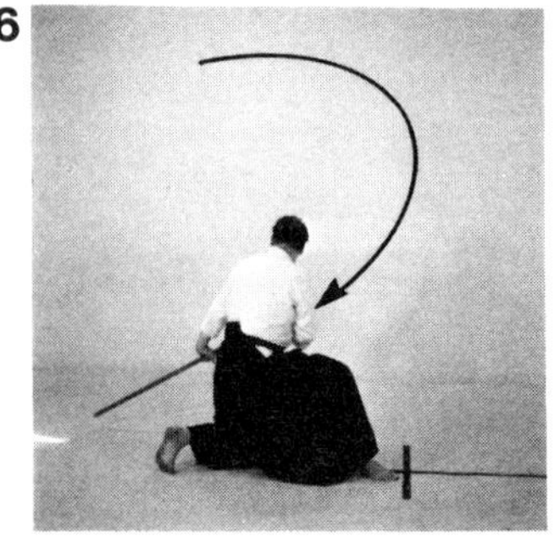

Fig. 250 A kneeling rear thrust. (This is a straight thrust and not a circular reap.)

Fig. 251 Rise, advance your left foot, and . . .

17

Fig. 252 Sweep to your opponent's ankle.

18

Fig. 253 Jab backhand to the top of his foot.

Fig. 254 Release your right hand, turn the jo end-over-end, . . .

Fig. 255 Regrip, and . . .

19

Fig. 256 Thrust underhand to his knee.

Fig. 257 Retreat and withdraw the jo in preparation for a . . .

20

Fig. 258 Retreating overhand sweep to his head. (Cap the end of the jo with your left palm at the end of the withdrawal.)

Fig. 259 Release your left hand and let the end drop.

Fig. 260 Turn the jo end-over-end, and . . .

21

Fig. 261 Thrust underhand to his chest.

Fig. 262 Roll into a . . .

22

Fig. 263 Left yokomen strike. This ends the kata.

Fig. 264 To repeat the kata from the beginning, hand-change and withdraw into a deflection.

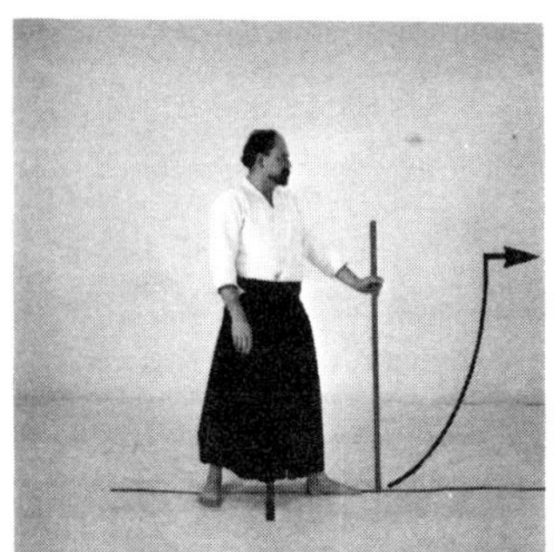
Fig. 265 Begin in sankakutai.

1

Fig. 266 Thrust overhand and . . .

2

Fig. 267 Deflect your opponent's jo to your right with a hooking motion.

3

Fig. 268 Drop out of the deflection and again thrust overhand.

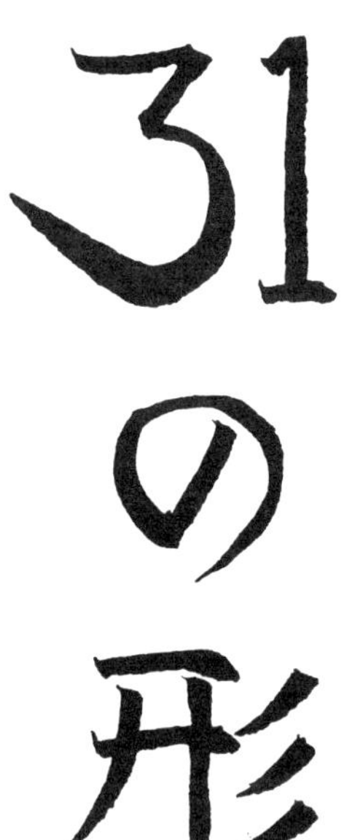

Kata No Sanjuichi

4

Fig. 269 Parry a counter-thrust to your left (the hand-change is the same as in suburi 2, although your grip is different) and continue into a . . .

5

Fig. 270 Right yokomen strike.

Fig. 271 Roll into a . . .

6

Fig. 272 Left yokomen strike.

Fig. 273 Lift your jo and pivot underneath it. The jo should not change direction during the pivot.

Fig. 274 From this modified jodan posture . . .

7

Fig. 275 Attack to the rear with a right yokomen strike.

8

Fig. 276 Roll into a left yokomen strike and continue turning into. . .

Fig. 277 A beating rear strike.

9

Fig. 278 At the end of the strike (which is the waka no kamae posture) . . .

10

Fig. 279 Walk forward with your right foot and beat his jo upward.

Fig. 280 Roll into . . .

11

Fig. 281 A left yokomen strike. Change the position of your left hand and move immediately into a . . .

12

FRONT VIEW

Fig. 282 Downward deflection (push your jo down with your fingers, right foot back).

13

Fig. 283 Rise from the deflection and thrust underhand.

14

Fig. 284 Parry a counter-thrust to your left, hand-change, and . . .

15

Fig. 285 Walk forward into a right yokomen strike.

Fig. 286 Withdraw the jo and . . .

16

Fig. 287 Thrust underhand to the rear.

17

Fig. 288 Walk forward with your left foot and sweep to his ankle.

18

Fig. 289 Release your right hand, let the end of the jo drop, and turn it end-over-end.

FRONT VIEW

Fig. 290 Deflect his jo down to the right and sweep your left foot to the right.

19

Fig. 291 Jab to his knee.

Fig. 292 Quickly rise into a hand-change (as in a deflection) and . . .

20

Fig. 293 Strike to his knee with a right yokomen strike as you step back with your left foot and begin to kneel.

Fig. 294 Continue kneeling while you withdraw the jo through your right hand to . . .

21

Fig. 295 Thrust to the rear while kneeling.

Fig. 296 Rise and advance and . . .

22

Fig. 297 Deliver a reverse-hand thrust to his face.

23

Fig. 298 Release your right hand and turn the jo end-over-end.

FRONT VIEW

Fig. 299 Regrip, and deflect his jo down (step back with your left foot).

24

Fig. 300 Return your left foot and thrust underhand.

FRONT VIEW

Fig. 301 Then push the butt of your jo down (to lift the end) and parry a thrust to your right.

25

Fig. 302 Lift the butt of your jo (as opposed to lowering the end) and thrust underhand.

Fig. 303 Withdraw the jo with your right hand.

26

Fig. 304 Shift your weight to your back foot, and . . .

27

Fig. 305 Deliver a reverse-hand sweep to his knee.

Fig. 306 Lift your jo and . . .

Fig 307 Jab backhand to his face.

29

Fig. 308 Release your left hand and turn the jo end-over-end.

FRONT VIEW

Fig. 309 Regrip, drop the end, and lift your knee to pass his sweep under your foot.

30

Fig. 310 Thrust underhand, and . . .

Fig. 311 Roll into a . . .

31

Fig. 312 Left yokomen strike. This ends the kata.

Fig. 313 To repeat the kata from the beginning, hand-change, and withdraw into a deflection.

GLOSSARY

ai harmony (from *au*: to meet).

aikido the way of harmonizing spiritual strength. A martial art that emphasizes leading and holding and that uses large flowing motions to throw an opponent.

aikijo harmonizing spiritual strength with a four-foot staff.

atemi attacks to vital points on the body of an opponent to disable him.

bo a staff, usually six feet in length. Short for *rokushaku bo.*

bu section.

choku front; direct.

chudan no kamae the middle stance of the traditional fencing postures.

do a method or way; a discipline and philosophy with both moral and spiritual implications.

gaeshi a turning to the outside (from *kaesu*: to turn out).

gedan no kamae the low stance of the traditional fencing postures.

gyaku reverse; opposite.

hachi eight.

hanbo a three-foot staff; literally, a half *bo.*

harai a beating away (from *harau*: to beat).

hasso no kamae a traditional fencing posture in which the weapon is held vertically above the right shoulder.

hidari left (the direction).

iaido the (martial) way of drawing and cutting with the Japanese sword.

ipon the number one; first. Expressed as *dai ipon.*

irimi an entering movement (from *ireru*: to put inside).

ji a figure, as in a Japanese character or *kanji.*

jo a four-foot staff.

jodan no kamae the high stance of the traditional fencing postures.

jodo the (martial) way of training with the four-foot staff.

jujutsu a traditional Japanese form of unarmed combat emphasizing throwing, joint locking, choking, and grappling techniques; literally, "pliancy" or "strength through yielding."

kaeshi same as *gaeshi*: a turning to the outside.

kamae a stance.

kata a long exercise or form; single.

katate single-hand.

ki spiritual strength.

kumijo sparring with a four-foot staff.

kyusho vital points on the body. See also *atemi.*

maai distance; the awareness of distance between oneself and one's opponent.

makiwara a target used for training.

men the head; face.

menuchi a strike to the head.

migi right (the direction).

nagare a flowing (from *nagareru*: to flow).

naginata halberd; a pole arm with a long, curved blade.

nipon two; second. Expressed as *dai nipon.*

randori free-style sport combat (from *randoru*: to spar).

renzoku consecutive strikes.

sankakutai a T-stance; here, a posture for the jo in which the forward hand holds the jo vertical, butt on the ground. Literally, "three-corner body."

shomen the top of the head.

suburi a short practice exercise.

suki an opening (for an attack).

toma long; far.

tsuki a thrust (from *tsukeru*: to thrust).

uchi a strike or cutting blow (from *utsu*: to strike).

uchikomi striking techniques.

ushiro behind; from the rear.

waka no kamae a traditional fencing posture in which the weapon is pointed back along one's right side.

waza technique; a way of doing something.

yari a spear.

yokomen the side of the head.

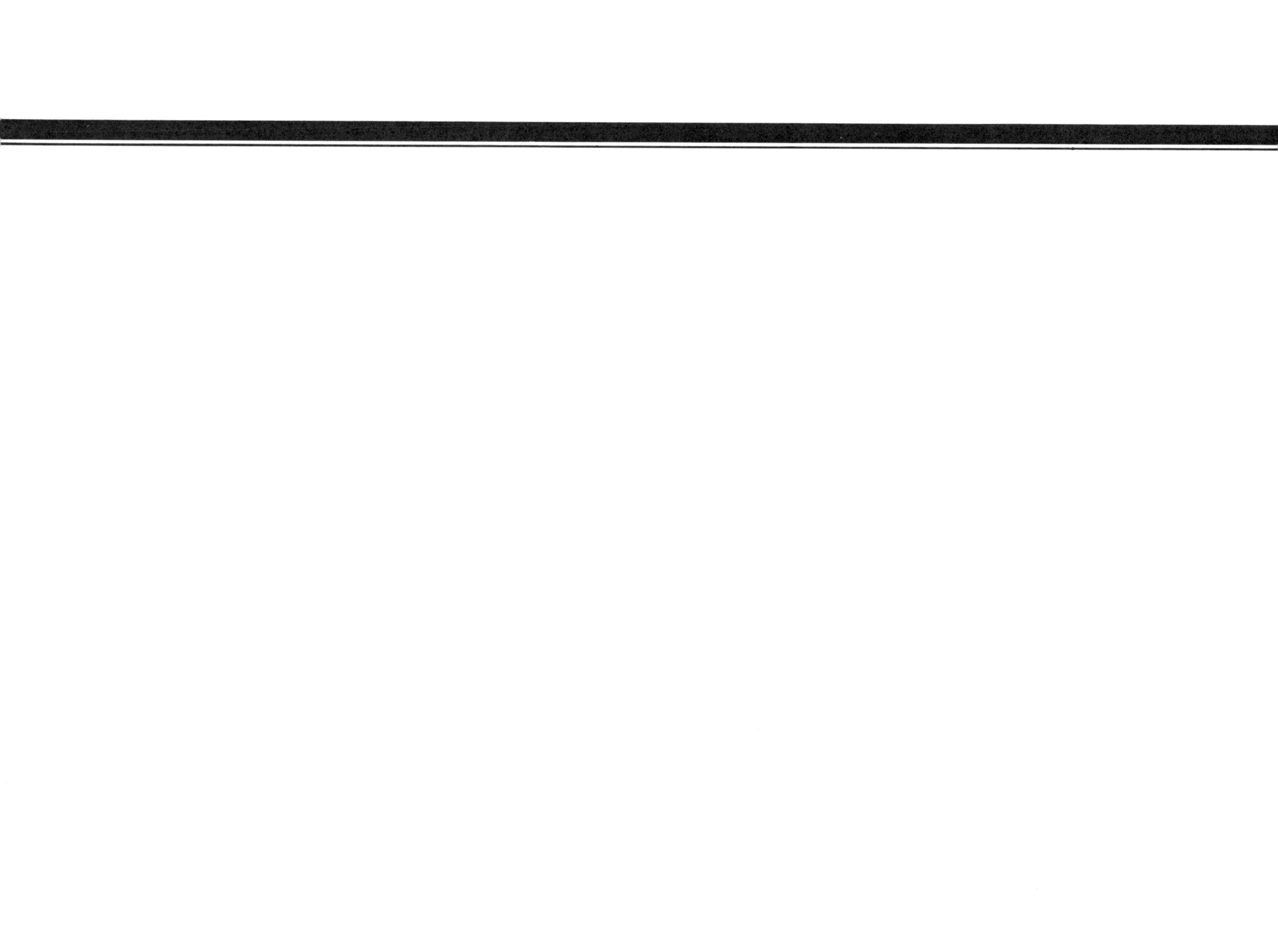

AFTERWORD

This book is intended to be an introductory text on the Japanese short staff. It is not a history, philosophy, or record of any specific martial art dedicated to the use of the jo. Rather, it is a collection of traditional training forms chosen from several martial arts. We feel this approach is preferable in an introductory text, and we hope this book will create or renew interest in the jo and the forms associated with it.

We have not addressed the spiritual or philosophical aspects that accompany the use of the jo in some martial arts. This is most notable in the absence of any reference to *ki,* or spiritual energy. All instructors approach this training with different methods and vocabularies. We have not included ours to give them space for their own.

The essence of the jo is dynamic, flowing movement that cannot be captured in posed photographs. Neither can this essence be described, no matter how carefully one selects the words. And not even competent instruction, carefully given can produce the insights that come from the personal experience of studying these forms.

ABOUT THE AUTHORS

Don Zier holds a third-degree black belt in *omoi ryu iaido* (the art of drawing and cutting with the sword), a second-degree black belt in *genseikan aikijutsu,* and a first-degree black belt in *shindo muso ryu jodo,* (the art of fighting with the four-foot staff). In addition, he has trained withthe *yari* (spear), *naginata* (halberd), and *hanbo* (three-foot staff). He now devotes most of his time to *kyudo* (the art of drawing the bow). A martial artist for over 35 years, he has studied extensively in the Pacific Northwest and Japan and continues to practice daily. He is the director of a university computer center.

Tom Lang holds a third-degree black belt in *dan zan ryu (kodenkan) jujutsu* and two second-degree black belts in *muso shinden ryu iaido.* He has studied the sword, staff, and spear with Mr. Zier since 1973. Under several instructors, he has trained in aikido, iaido, the Filipino martial arts of kali, escrima, and arnis, and the police arts of the straight baton, the side-handle baton, and the riot baton. He is a technical writer and author in the fields of medicine and health.